WIMBLEDON
2008

Winner of The Rolex Wimbledon Picture of the Year Competition 2008
Photographer: FELIPE TRUEBA of EPA

THE CHAMPIONSHIPS
WIMBLEDON
OFFICIAL ANNUAL
2008

NEIL HARMAN

Publisher
PPL Sport & Leisure

Managing Director
Bill Cotton

Art Editor
David Kelly

Design Team
Emma Robinson
Graham Nuttall
Caroline O'Donovan

Photography
PA Photos

Editorial
Neil Harman

Editorial Liaison
Kevin McGoverin

Copyright (c) 2008
The All England Lawn Tennis
and Croquet Club

Photographs Copyright (c)
PA Photos

This edition
published 2008 by
PPL Sport & Leisure
16 Dempster Building
Atlantic Way
Brunswick Business Park
Liverpool L3 4BE

PPL Sport & Leisure
Bradford House
East Street
Epsom, Surrey KT17 1BL

ISBN 978-1-903381-18-2

Printed by Viva Press
Barcelona

No part of this publication may be
reproduced, stored in a retrieval
system or transmitted in any form
or by any means electronic,
mechanical, photocopying,
recording or otherwise without
prior permission in writing from
PPL Sport & Leisure.

Results tables are reproduced
courtesy of the All England Lawn
Tennis and Croquet Club.

This book is reproduced with the
assistance of Rolex.

CONTENTS

FOREWORD
Tim Phillips
Chairman of The All England Lawn Tennis and Croquet Club
and Committee of Management of The Championships

If Rod Laver, Bjorn Borg, John McEnroe and Boris Becker all think the 2008 men's single final was the greatest match ever played at Wimbledon, then it is safe to assume it was.

For the third consecutive year Roger Federer was challenged in the Wimbledon final by Rafael Nadal. The top two players in the world (many think the two best players ever) battled for over $4^3/4$ hours in one of all sports greatest contests before the Spaniard eventually triumphed to win his first Wimbledon just four weeks after defending his French Open title – only the third man to do this double in the Open era.

This amazing final, punctuated by two rain delays, had everything. Federer fought back from two sets down to come within two points of retaining his title. And we had thought that the wonderful Andy Murray versus Richard Gasquet match in the quarter-final would be the match of the tournament as Andy recovered from a two set deficit to triumph in the fifth set!

In the ladies' singles we had a family Williams final for the third time. In fact, in the twenty first century either or both Venus and Serena have been in the final every year but one. This final was a superb competitive match between the two big hitting sisters – comfortably the best quality match they have ever played against each other. Later that evening the two sisters returned to Centre Court to win the ladies' doubles – without having lost a set in the tournament.

In the men's doubles Jonas Bjorkman, playing his sixteenth and last Wimbledon (and partnered by Kevin Ullyett) just failed to add to his three Wimbledon doubles titles when they were defeated by Daniel Nestor and Nenad Zimonjic in four sets. This final was also remarkable for the fact Nenad played with a fractured left arm (the radius bone) sustained in a fall earlier in the tournament.

And the above simply outlines the finals! Within this 2008 Wimbledon Annual you will find the full story of the 122nd Championships. I hope you enjoy it. ●

INTRODUCTION
Neil Harman, The Times

At around 4pm on the day before the 122nd Championships, looking out of the window of the Press Centre, it was very evident that whereas players tend to make their way along St Mary's Walk with a purposeful stride back and forth to the practice courts at Aorangi Park, this time they were dashing past, heads covered with towels. And not just the players – everyone was dashing hither and thither in a right old two an' eight.

A glance upwards and we immediately knew why. The sky had darkened but this was no herald of an imminent cloudburst. There was a swarm of bees, hundreds of the little devils, circling, diving, making an utter nuisance of themselves. Apparently, the queen had been disturbed in a nearby nest, all the bees had lost their bearings and the upshot was complete pandemonium. Fortunately, the Club called someone who deals with these things, a squirt or two of some nasty spray and they had dispersed.

It did not usually take much to get Wimbledon all a-buzz but here we had it. And who, in the following fortnight, would be the victim of a sting? The Championship build up had been even more remarkable than normal. On the men's side, Rafael Nadal had humbled Roger Federer in the final of the French Open, capturing his fourth consecutive title on the clay of Roland Garros without dropping a set. Not only that, he had gone on to defeat a world class field in the Artois championships at Queen's Club. Federer had not done so badly himself, taking the grass court title in Halle for the fifth time in six years, this without dropping serve.

I was fortunate to have had an appointment with the five time champion a couple of days prior to the raising of the curtain. He had decided to limit media appearances this time around, saying he had done enough in the year's past and didn't want to wear himself out unduly. The question was – how did one broach Paris – come straight out with it or butter him up a little and then drop the question in? I decided to go for the latter.

With that, Federer slipped into one of the Club's superior sofas and if your expectation was of finding someone whose mind had been turned to mush after the worst performance in terms of games won by a world No.1 in the history of grand slam tournament finals, who had been beaten by slavering critics, or was concerned that he is about to become the victim of a lawn mowing, you were in the wrong place at the wrong time with the wrong man.

The greeting was warm, the eye contact immediate. He knew what you were thinking and you knew he knew what you were thinking. He wanted to drink in his surroundings first. He was dressed head to toe in white, the RF hat dispensed with, nothing to hide. He was enjoying being a tour guide to Gary Hamilton, his Australian fitness trainer, the newest member of Team Fed. "I realise for me, this is a very, very special place and it's nice to pass those feelings on to somebody else," he said.

"I came here first in the juniors, in 1998, when I was one of so many but now I am *the* one." He knows his place, does the man. "Winning the singles title once was incredible because this is Wimbledon, the most important, and then two became three and then four and then five, and five is definitely a different league again. Six would be extraordinary and I have a great opportunity."

OK, that was enough beating around the bush. Was he not hurt, devastated, was he not less of a less of a player after Paris? "Well, I've come from Halle where I didn't drop serve and that was only the second time in my career with Doha that that has happened," he said, disarming once more. "I decided straight after the French final I wanted to go there. Normally I sleep on a decision like that but it wasn't as if the final had been particularly tough, it was over so quickly. I'd felt physically fine throughout the tournament. I was over it fast."

Really? "Rafa was outplaying me in the first set and he has the ability to do that on the clay, in the second I had a good start but he fought back. I had a small chance but when he is up two sets to love, he does not waste time. I didn't think at the start it would happen the way it did, but it did happen and it's 'oh well, what the hell.'

"Rafa will be the favourite in Paris for years to come but why should I not believe I can beat him. A player who has won 12 grand slams can never go into a final thinking 'what's the point?' I never will. On any given day, on any surface, against any player, I am the favourite to win. I felt I had him figured out, the conditions were in my favour, but it wasn't meant to be. What am I supposed to do?"

Nadal's reaction to his victory was splendidly respectful and brief. "He could have rolled around for ten minutes if he'd wanted to, I would not have had a problem with that, seriously," Federer said. "It was *his* moment. The problem of a win like that is that he had seen it coming for half an hour, 45 minutes before, and he probably felt he could not beat Roger Federer by this score so it was an awkward situation for him. He almost didn't dare to celebrate too much."

The response to the size of Federer's defeat was eerie. Ex-champions who sang his praises before the final then fell silent. The wordsmiths were cutting in the extreme. Rather than condemn too swiftly, Federer preferred a healthy dose of perspective. "The thing I have never felt comfortable with this year has been the glandular fever and how I reacted to it," he said. "What was the best time to say I had not been well in Australia (where he lost in the semi-finals to Novak Djokovic). I wasn't sure if I should say anything at all, should I say something in Dubai, perhaps after I had won a title – what was the best time? For me, it wasn't fun to be hiding something, people asking me in Dubai (the tournament after Australia) – 'how are you feeling?' and me answering 'fine'.

Eventually, after he had lost to Andy Murray in the first round in Dubai, Federer decided to go public. "Perhaps people did not believe me, but why should I lie?" he said. "Some might say I lost to Novak in Melbourne because of that but it was not the reason at all. He outplayed me in the semi-final and I have no problems accepting that. There were those who said it was a little excuse and others said 'oh, now it all makes sense.'

"When I lost in the semi-finals of Indian Wells and the quarters of Miami, everyone said I was going downhill but no account was taken of what I had gone through. I suppose I had not given anyone a chance to criticise me for four years and they would want to take that chance.

"That is past, this is the most important time. The period after the French, with Wimbledon, the Olympics Games and the US Open, that is when this season will be decided for me, whether it has been better or worse. If I haven't won any of those titles then I will agree that this year has not been up to my standards. But let's wait and see what happens. Why do people want to shoot me so soon?" I let that one rest.

The loss of Justine Henin to world tennis had come as a complete shock – a few days before the French Open, which she had won in four of the previous five years, the Belgian announced that her stellar career was at an end. It was difficult to believe that the two time Wimbledon runner-up would never have the chance of completing her grand slam title collection. All the fight had gone from her, she said, and she preferred now to concentrate on an academy in Limelette, 30 miles from Brussels, where she hoped to find plenty of Henins for the future.

Ana Ivanovic, the 20-year-old from Serbia was, therefore, the top seed and world No.1 entering Wimbledon for the first time and a grand slam champion to boot, having won the French title in a dramatic final against Russia's Dinara Safina.

There had been some confusion before the tournament about the allocation of singles wild cards – two British men, Jamie Baker and Alex Bogdanovic, had managed to sneak into the draw as they were inside the LTA's cut-off ranking of No.250 when the relevant committee came to review the situation. Only four wild cards were given into the men's event – a first – the British pair plus Xavier Malisse, of Belgium, a former semi-finalist, and Jeremy Chardy of France, the 2005 boys champion. In the women's main draw, there were the usual eight wild cards, four British girls plus Zheng Jie of China, Australia's Samantha Stosur, Urszula Radwanska of Poland and Spain's Carla Suarez Navarro, who had qualified and reached the quarter-finals at Roland Garros.

And Tim Henman was back – the newest member of the BBC's commentary team. We would be doting on his every word.

Around the grounds much had altered and though nothing ever seemed to *really* change – an All England Club speciality, that. A permanent non-moveable new roof was in place on Centre Court after the previous year's bare appearance. There were more seats – 15,000, as opposed to 13,800 in 2007; the new Court 2 was structurally complete and on schedule for use in 2009; Court 13 had been demolished and Court 11 would be the new show court in the southernmost tip of the grounds. The facilities for the Debenture Holders (those who paid for these astonishing developments) had taken a significant turn for the better – they had a Tea Lawn, a Long Bar, The Terrace, the Wingfield Restaurant, a Champagne Bar, Skyview Suites and a Roof Top Bar. Anyone for tennis?   ●

Roger Federer
Seeded 1st

Age: 26. Born: Basel, Switzerland.

The 1998 Boys' champion, who had lost in the first round on his three of his first four appearances in the main draw, Federer was now the most accomplished player in the world, an artist, whose shot-making and style were the talk of the sport. After last year's Championships, when he equalled Bjorn Borg's five successive Gentleman's singles titles, he had gone on to lift the US Open title and the Masters Cup but the start to 2008 had been a disappointment for someone of such exemplary standards. He had won just two minor titles and had been heavily beaten by Rafael Nadal in the final of the French Open, winning just four games.

Rafael Nadal
Seeded 2nd

Age: 22. Born: Manacor, Majorca.

The beaten Wimbledon finalist for the past two years, Nadal's preparation for The Championships had been extraordinary. He had won the clay court titles in Monte Carlo, Barcelona, Hamburg and rounded off the season winning the French Open for the fourth year in succession without dropping a set. Coming straight to London on the Eurostar after his triumph at Roland Garros, he then landed the Artois tournament at the Queen's Club - and no one in history had managed that clay/grass court title combination without a week of rest in between. After a few days home in Majorca to replenish and rest, he was ready to challenge for the title he believed was his destiny.

Novak Djokovic
Seeded 3rd

Age: 21. Born: Belgrade, Serbia.

Djokovic was now clearly part of a triumverate that had separated themselves from the rest of the men's game. Having reached the final of the 2007 US Open, Djokovic really announced himself on the world stage by taking the Australian Open title, beating Federer in the semi-finals and Jo-Wilfried Tsonga of France in an exuberant, no-holds barred final in Melbourne. Not only that, Djokovic had won two Masters titles, on hard courts, in Indian Wells, California and on clay, in Rome. A fiercely proud Serbian, he was eagerly talking up his Wimbledon prospects and wanted desperately to erase from his memory last year's semi-final when he was forced to quit with blistered feet against Nadal.

Nikolay Davydenko
Seeded 4th

Age: 27. Born: Severodonezk, Ukraine.

If the top three had opened up a gap between themselves and the rest, then Nikolay Davydenko, the Russian baseliner, had become something of an immoveable world No.4. His year, thus far, had been highlighted by victory in the Sony Ericsson Open in Miami, beating Rafael Nadal in the final. Davydenko had won two clay court tournaments, in Warsaw and Portschach, Austria but had declined to play any grass court tennis in the Wimbledon build-up. He had worked hard on developing his game and his personality, though he suffered still from a terrible shyness.

David Ferrer
Seeded 5th

Age: 26. Born: Javea, Spain.

He was becoming the there or thereabouts man in men's tennis, always in the thick of tournaments but tending to stumble at the last minute. The exception had come this year in Valencia, on clay (a tournament in which he beat five fellow Spaniards to win) and, remarkably, the week before The Championships, he won the grass court title at Rosmalen, Holland which was a notable first. Ferrer, one of the quickest players around, had reached the semi-finals of a grand slam tournament for the first time at the 2007 US Open, which helped him qualify for the Masters Cup, where he was beaten in the final by Roger Federer.

Andy Roddick
Seeded 6th

Age: 25. Born: Omaha, Nebraska, USA.

Having decided to stop working with Jimmy Connors, his coach, at the end of 2007, it was going to be intriguing to see how this engaging American, who had helped his country to Davis Cup victory over France in fabulous style, would fare. His season began with a hurtful loss to Germany's Philipp Kohlschreiber in the third round of the Australian Open and though he defeated Rafael Nadal and Novak Djokovic en route to the Dubai Open the following month, his spring had been interrupted by a shoulder spasm injury he picked up in the semi-finals of the Rome Masters. Wimbledon remained the title he wanted to win above all others.

David Nalbandian
Seeded 7th

Age: 26. Born: Cordoba, Argentina.

The end of 2007 had been a period of sustained success for the 2002 Wimbledon runner-up. He won two indoor Masters tournaments in succession, in Madrid, where he beat Roger Federer in the final and, two weeks later, in Paris, where Rafael Nadal was his victim. It was seen as a defining moment for the Argentinian and yet he had not moved ahead much in 2008, winning his home title in Buenos Aires but failing to trouble the scorers through the spring clay court run - where his second round loss to Jeremy Chardy of France at Roland Garros - was particularly humbling. He had lost 6-0, 6-1 to Novak Djokovic in the semi-finals of the Artois championships.

Richard Gasquet
Seeded 8th

Age: 22. Born: Beziers, France.

It had been a particularly tough year for the young Frenchman with the splendid game and ever so silky backhand. There had not been a single tournament semi-final on his resume, indeed his only quarter-final appearance came at Queen's Club where he lost to David Nalbandian. To make matters worse, he had been roundly criticised by his home nation for declining to play in the first Davis Cup singles on the third day of the final against Andy Roddick, the previous December. For someone who took criticism so much hard, these were daunting times. But he loved the grass, as his semi-final appearance in SW19 last year had amply demonstrated.

Ana Ivanovic
Seeded 1st

Age: 20. Born: Belgrade, Serbia.

First played Wimbledon as a 17-year-old, reached the fourth round as an 18-year-old and now, at 20, was the top seed and the No.1 player in the world. This delightful Serbian had won the French Open two weeks earlier, breaking her grand slam tournament duck after twice being a runner-up, in Paris a year earlier and Melbourne in January. In between those, she had won the prestigious Pacific Life Open in Indian Wells, California. Clearly, all the parts of her game were beginning to add up, she gave the ball a mighty clip from the ground and did everything with a smile which was, indeed, a rarity.

Jelena Jankovic
Seeded 2nd

Age: 23. Born: Belgrade, Serbia.

There was obviously something in the Belgrade air for here was the second seed coming from the same birthplace as the No.1 and that happened once every blue moon. Jankovic had been taken to British hearts by combining with Jamie Murray to win the mixed doubles title in 2007. She had made a habit of being a semi-finalist this year (it happened in four tournaments) besides which she had won the Italian Open, on clay, and been beaten in the final, of Miami, on hard courts, by Serena Williams in three tough sets. Was a little injury and illness prone and an inveterate user of Kleenex.

Maria Sharapova

Seeded 3rd

Age: 21. Born: Nyagan, Russia.

It was hard to credit that Sharapova was still just 21, considering how long she had been a permanent attraction on the circuit. She had collected her third grand slam title with the Australian Open falling her way in January and had won further tournaments in Doha and Amelia Island, having stopped off on the way back from Australia to play a Fed Cup tie for her home nation in Israel, which provoked a flurry of interest. She had not had a particularly memorable clay court season and looked in need of sharpness coming into The Championships but had to be considered among the favourites, given her liking for the grass.

Svetlana Kuznetsova

Seeded 4th

Age: 22. Born: St Petersburg, Russia.

Her US Open triumph in 2004 had been the one and only time the Russian had delivered completely on her talents, though she nearly came close again in New York last September, losing the final to Justine Henin. 2007 was to prove the best of her career in which she reached No.2 in the Sony Ericsson WTA Tour rankings. Though she possessed thumping groundstrokes, and a lioness's courage, she had reached three finals in 2008, in Sydney, Indian Wells and Dubai but had no titles to her credit and had been beaten in the first round of Eastbourne, by Carloine Wozniacki, of Poland.

Elena Dementieva
Seeded 5th

Age: 26. Born: Moscow, Russia.

She was having an extremely consistent year, with finals in Dubai, Berlin and Istanbul and semi-finals at the Paris Indoors, Charleston and Rosmalen, but nothing of a trophy-lifting variety yet for the blonde from Moscow, a two-time grand slam tournament runner-up (though those were both in 2004, some time ago). There was something a good deal more solid in her game, too, her serve had come on in leaps and bounds, she was as strong as anyone off the ground and you felt if she could only conquer her nerves, she could win something very big one day.

Serena Williams
Seeded 6th

Age: 26. Born: Saginaw, Michigan, USA.

It was now 18 months since Serena Williams had won a grand slam title – the Australian Open in 2007, her eighth overall – and her shock, straight sets, third round defeat to Katarina Srebotnik, of Slovenia, in the French Open made one wonder quite whether she was properly prepared for The Championships. She had won the Sony Ericsson Open title in Miami as she tended to do on her home patch (actually for the fifth time) but, then again, something raised the Williams sisters at this time of year, she said that there was nothing to worry about and you usually took her at her word.

Venus Williams

Seeded 7th

Age: 28. Born: Lynwood, California, USA.

Like her sister, Serena, Venus had lost in the third round of the French Open – to Italy's Flavia Pennetta in her case – and so no one quite knew what to expect, even from someone who had won Wimbledon twice in the previous three years and four times in all. Considering she had begun 2007 ranked No.48 and completed it ranked No.8 and that her game had not really changed at all in shape and texture from when she burst onto the scene here 11 years ago, she would have as good a chance as anyone of lifting the trophy. A calm descended on her at this time of year and she was seeded 16 places higher than she was at last year's Championships.

Anna Chakvetadze

Seeded 8th

Age: 21. Born: Moscow, Russia.

This was to be her 14th tournament of the season, so no one could criticise the Moscovite from shirking the work required to keep up her world ranking. In 2007, she had ended the year inside the top 10 for the first time, marking that with a semi-final appearance at the US Open, her first such performance at a grand slam. Had never been beyond the third round in SW19 and little she had done, so far, in 2008 suggested she was about to set the world alight. She had won the Paris Indoor title back in February and reached the semi-finals in Rome on clay but otherwise her record was a lot of matches and not enough times contending for titles.

Court
19

Day **ONE**
23.06.2008

KARLOVIC
VS
STADLER

NALBANDIAN
VS
DANCEVIC

ONDRASKOVA
VS
VAIDISOVA

CIBULKOVA
VS
ZHENG JIE

FEDERER
VS
HRBATY

BAGHDATIS
VS
DARCIS

Ian Ritchie, the chief executive of the All England Club, had begun to think he was a curse. In his first two years in the job, the first Monday of The Championships had been tantamount to a washout, nothing but dark clouds and even darker dispositions. "The same is true of Andrew Jarrett, our referee; he's not had a clear first day since he took over," Ritchie said, trying to shift the blame. "When are we going to see some sun?"

Belatedly on the first day of 2008, as Ritchie was being interviewed on the balcony near the referee's office by a Japanese television station, it was clear that both his days as the chief rainmaker had gone and that he had not been raiding the Club's supply of Factor 20. His forehead was becoming a deepish shade of red. Oh, blessed, blessed day.

It is remarkable how everyone's mood changes when the sun is out. The ground staff mow the lawns dressed in short-sleeved shirts rather than the usual wind-cheaters, some of them even whistle a happy tune as they go. Happiness abounds. We meet and greet old friends and get used to the rhythms of The Championships in a great mood, one helped by walking down from Wimbledon Village where they were having to water the plant pots from cans rather than leaving it to the waterfall belonging to the Big Man in the Heavens.

A few clouds scudded by but they did not linger long. The weather seemed set fair. For one day, two, perhaps even four, there was no sign of rain in the forecast. It had been pretty glorious through the qualifying competition at Roehampton as well. Wimbledon remains the only one of the four grand slam tournaments where the qualifying competition took place at a venue which is not the site for The Championships themselves and there was something uniquely quaint about that.

The lead story of the 'qualies' as they are universally known was that a British player, Chris Eaton, had won his way through in circumstances a trifle bizarre. Having lost in the semi-finals of an LTA wild card play-off, the fact that two other British players landed spots in the Slazenger Nottingham Open freed up places in the qualifying draw. Eaton was called back, won three matches and defeated Olivier Patience, of France, ranked over 500 spots above him, in the final round, serving 31 aces in the process. Roehampton rocked.

So we had new names to write about, new ideas to generate, new heroes to admire. As we walked in on day one, the courts pristine, the weather beguiling, we wondered what the fates had in store, because, on a daily basis at Wimbledon, something happened that set your pulse rate on edge. Everyone had had ➢

their say in the build-up and a lot of folk thought that Ivo Karlovic, the giant Croatian, who had just won the Nottingham Open for the second year in succession, was a player to be avoided at all costs.

At 6'10", like a skyscraper with a racket, he was a fearsome sight and yet The Championships had not been particularly kind to him. How was it that the man who had dethroned Lleyton Hewitt, the defending champion, in the first round of 2003, had then blazed a losing trail in the succeeding first rounds, succumbing to folks such as Daniele Bracciali of Italy, Stanislas Wawrinka of

David Nalbandian

Dominika Cibulkova

Switzerland and, in 2007, to Fabrice Santoro who lobbed him on a service return to win that match on Court 5 – one of the most audacious shots I had ever witnessed.

Karlovic was up against Simon Stadler, of Germany, a left hander one recalled from his victory over Alex Bogdanovic, the British No.3, in qualifying for the Australian Open in January. Stadler had plenty of dextrous shots but would surely not delay Karlovic. How wrong one was as the slight Stadler won 4-6 7-6 6-3 7-5. Also gone from the men's singles was David Nalbandian, who had not been able to live up to his 2002 final and quarter-final a couple of years later.

Who knew how the Argentinian ticked? A player who could win the two premier European indoor Masters Series tournaments in Madrid and Paris back to back at the end of last year – defeating Roger Federer in one and Rafael Nadal in the other – was surely equipped to handle anything. Then one remembered his depressing semi-final

performance in the Artois championships at Queen's, when he won a single game against Novak Djokovic and ought to have been ashamed to collect his prize money.

His exchange, after his 6-4 6-2 6-4 defeat to Frank Dancevic of Canada on No.1 court, was as brief as the match itself. Q. Physically you're fine? There was no problem with that? Did you feel your preparation was good? Nalbandian: Well, not a hundred percent, but...Q. In what way? Nalbandian: Injuries. Q. What's the injury? Nalbandian: I can't tell you. Q. Why? Nalbandian: I have to? Q: No. Nalbandian: All right. Over and out.

Though he was not the first to depart. Of course, one of the big story lines, on the first Monday, was noting the first player to head for the prize money office to collect their £10,250. Step forward – if that is the appropriate term – one Zuzana Ondraskova of the Czech Republic. Her departure heralded a brief flaunting of emotion. She rolled her eyes at the umpire, raged expressively with her hands, picked up her bag and set about finding the quickest way home to Prague. She has played in the tournament five times and not won a match. Her very quick sets were 22 minutes and 22. The taxi ride to Heathrow would take longer.

Ondraskova did pause long enough to talk about her Eastern European origins. The same subject was touched upon by the second fastest loser, Ioana Raluca Olaru, of Romania (67 minutes and out) and the first seed to fall, Dominika Cibulkova, the No.30 seed from Slovakia (86 minutes). One might have thought that first-round capitulation in one of the year's four grand-slam tournaments would represent a traumatic day at the office. However, no one appeared to be bearing disappointment as too great a weight. Cibulkova explained that she had been carrying an injury and was unable to prepare on grass. Olaru said that she was not due to fly out until Friday, that she wanted to see Big Ben and that she may see a bit of her sister, who works in London in IT.

They all also touched on the ever-increasing predominance of Eastern Europeans at the peak of their sport and explained that it was something about the hardness of their background and the lack of other opportunities that accounted for their success. Given the meekness and the speed of their collective surrender on the grass, and their ability to come to terms with it, this was clearly – and unintentionally – deeply ironic.

The departure of those we did not really know, was being measured against the arrival of the man who was the talk of the tournament – Federer, the world No.1 and defending champion. As tradition demanded, ➤

Dominik Hrbaty and Roger Federer

he was first up on Centre Court against Dominik Hrbaty, the veteran Slovakian, who had won their only two meetings and, when he saw Federer practise the day before the event began, had wondered if his record frightened the champion at all. Federer then played three successive shots that made Hrbaty gulp. Even so, he could not make it a hat-trick, could he? Simon Barnes, in *The Times* was concerned more with all things fashion. The Federer cardigan, of which 230 had been minted to celebrate said number of weeks as the world No.1, was drawing critical acclaim. "It's a little bit more easy to wear than the jacket," Federer said when this most important topic was ventilated.

Barnes wrote: "Certainly, this will be an important chapter in the doctoral-length thesis on Great Woollies of Wimbledon, but I can think of two better. The first is the sleeveless jumper worn by Jeremy Bates in 1992, when he reached the fourth round, punching well above his weight, while wearing a woolly to protect a poorly shoulder. But, alas, he took it off in the fourth round and so, inevitably, he lost to Guy Forget (of France). The Wimbledon woolly of all time, though, is the pink cardy worn by Virginia Wade when she won the women's singles in 1977 – surely the woolly of all woollies. Federer's cardy has some way to go if it is to match the little pink job.

"But as cardies go, it started out the right way. Federer reeled off the first 11 points, prompting speculation that he would be the first man to win Wimbledon without losing a point. Back on Centre Court, he looked as if he had turned back into Rodge again. The man hagridden by worries, and by his self-imposed duty of pretending that he had no worries, seemed to have vanished."

Federer won in straight sets and perhaps the most memorable incident of the match arrived midway through the second set when Hrbaty decided he ought to sit on the chair next to Federer rather than that on the opposite side of the umpire's chair. The pair chatted amicably for a couple of minutes then resumed business. It was a lovely moment.

The French and the Japanese were not that concerned with outer garments. There had been plentiful words written in the build-up to the championships about the form and prospects of Gael Monfils and Kei Nishikori. Monfils, the former Wimbledon boys champion, had reached the semi-finals of the French Open, stirring his nation's passions and giving a fabulous account of himself against Federer at Roland Garros. There was plenty of marvel at, this angular, fluent ball striker, whose legs and body did not always move in harmony but who played delightfully intuitive tennis. Unfortunately, Monfils' right shoulder ➢

Marcos Baghdatis in action against Steve Darcis

QUOTE of the Day

Elena Baltacha – (Great Britain) after her 6-2 2-6 7-5 victory over Angelique Kerber, of Germany. "I added quite a bit of weight end of last year, you know, because of my back. I had other kind of problems and stuff. I wasn't fit. I went to Doha just before I moved to the National Tennis Centre and both my legs completely cramped up. I was in last round of qualifying, and at five-all I had to pull out because I just was in tears. My whole body just shut off. I knew I was unfit and I needed to do something about it. But the nutrition side, what I'm doing is knowing what to eat at what time, what food does what to your body, and how it affects you. I've trimmed down a lot. I feel really fit. Physically-wise I'm at my peak at the moment." Q. Have you had to cut anything out that you particularly like eating? "Yeah, pizza. I'm really gutted. I'm sure I can have it as a treat."

was hurting to such an extent that he had to withdraw without striking a ball and we had been denied seeing someone who, I supposed, would be among potential champions one year.

We saw not enough of Nishikori either. He had given Rafael Nadal an excellent match at Queen's Club, ten days earlier, but had been struggling since with a stomach muscle injury and, at one set all against Marc Gicquel of France, he decided he could play no further part. Japan sighed a very heavy sigh.

Cyprus, on the other hands, was in fine fettle. It was always good to see Marcos Baghdatis at his exuberant best and here he was on Court No.2, digging out a tough four

set victory over Steve Darcis, of Belgium, and reminding himself how fine a grass court exponent he was, with previous semi-final and quarter-final appearances. "It feels good to be playing back here," Baghdatis, who was now being coached by Peter Lundgren, the former Great Britain Davis Cup coach. "This is one of my favorite surfaces, if not my favorite one. For sure it feels good."

Of course, there were those who were sad to be leaving, for whatever reason, either bad luck, bad play or just a bad day at the office. But Day One had dawned, we saw it through without an interruption and heading back up the hill to the Village, everyone's garden looked particularly rosy. ●

Day **TWO**
24.06.2008

EATON
VS
PASHANSKI

CAVADAY
VS
V. WILLIAMS

KEOTHAVONG
VS
KING

DAVYDENKO
VS
BECKER

NADAL
VS
BECK

MURRAY
VS
SANTORO

BJORKMAN
VS
CLEMENT

Chris Eaton

Court No.3 at Wimbledon is one of those really nice places to watch tennis. You are able, if you so wish, to snuggle closely to the person in the next seat, you can stand on tip-toe on the stairs if you are not shoo-ed away by one of Wimbledon's splendid band of Honorary Stewards, who do shooing better than anyone else at any sports venue.

Of course, if you are a member of the Club, the balcony above the main entrance affords a wonderful view. How could it be better to watch tennis, with a cup of Earl Grey in one hand and a buttered scone in the other? Late afternoon on the first Tuesday of The Championships and the surrounds were packed, to watch the world No.661.

Chris Eaton was his name and he had become something of a talking point. After all, he had qualified through what John McEnroe had once described as the hardest event in the sport anywhere to succeed in. He was British and that always created an extra frisson of excitement, but the fact that no one had really heard of him before, made this an even more delightful story.

Eaton drove a battered Vauxhall Astra with duct tape holding together one of its wing mirrors and here he was, amid the Porsche and Bentley drivers of world tennis, the 128 lucky ones to have made the singles main draw, by virtue of his qualification successes. A first round against Boris Pashanski, a bullish Serbian who had played twice on grass in his life, and had lost both times, was one of those slices of fortune you prayed for.

The chances were that Pashanski would win, especially given the discrepancy in the world rankings but the crowd was intimately partisan – and there was nothing wrong with that. Eaton had a notable serve, a dreamy single handed backhand, a desire to attack the net and more backing than he had ever had in his life. The portents were favourable. And he did not let the side down.

Eaton defeated Pashanski 6-3 7-6 6-4, provoking widespread delirium. "It's going to help me travel around, to play the tournaments I want to play, to fund my life," Eaton said of the £17,000 he had secured by reaching the second round. "To win a match like this is phenomenal and the way I'd been serving, I knew I had a chance."

What, wondered the brilliant author Giles Smith, ought the All England Club do about such success? "The result inevitably pleased Eaton's parents, his coach and a noisy crowd that had stayed late into the evening, but it creates a steep alliterative challenge for those burdened with the renaming of Henman Hill that will have to happen, by default, if the Briton forces his way much farther. Over the years, the flexible grass vantage point has become Rusedski Ridge and Murray Mount, according to necessity, but, unfortunately, we may be running out of convenient geographical terms. 'Eaton Embankment' doesn't really cut the mustard. 'Eaton Escarpment' may be marginally worse. 'The Playing Field of Eaton'? Wrong signals, probably.

Boris Pashanski

Naomi Cavaday in action against Venus Williams

"Yesterday's was a victory worth marking, though. When he walked on, with slightly hunkered-down, purposeful shoulders, Eaton was ranked a distant No 661 in the world. No other player in the men's draw this year is ranked that deep. Of course, all British players at Wimbledon, by definition, are 'hopeful' and must be described as such in accordance with an ancient bylaw governing all published writing in connection with The Championships. But Eaton was, by a country mile, the most hopeful of all. Has there ever been a more hopeful Brit in round one?"

Eaton was not the only plucky one on show. A fabulous set against Venus Williams, the defending champion, did not mean that everything in Naomi Cavaday's garden was rosy, but the manner in which the Kentish girl took the game to the defending champion on Centre Court, serving with gusto and striking cross-court winners with courage and conviction, gave rise to optimism that she would not be lingering long at No.197 in the Sony Ericsson WTA Tour rankings.

Williams led 40-0 in the first game when she was interrupted by what she described later as 'a big old bumblebee' and was worried if they stung or not. Told afterwards that they did, just the once before that was their lot, she winced. Venus lost that service game and a few doubts began to buzz in her head. The champion's face was a study in flint as Cavaday stayed with her, stroke for stroke, until, at 5-4 down in the tie-break, the Briton netted her least composed backhand of the match. That was to be the end of her hopes, for Williams cantered away with it, winning 7-6, 6-1.

Asked what advice she would give to Cavaday, Venus suggested that she might get in touch with her father, Richard. "That would definitely help because he is a great coach," she said. "A lot of times you need someone to help you through those moments when you're too hard on yourself, to get you to that next level of positivity and confidence and good thoughts."

There was a real sense that such roots are beginning to take hold in more British women players. Anne Keothavong who had been the first from these shores — well, via Laos — to gain direct entry into the draw since Samantha Smith in 1999, defeated Vania King, of the United States, 4-6, 6-2, 6-3, and was already a leading contender for the award for the best toilet break of the championships. Having played a horrid first set, Keothavong took herself off for some relief and came back completely refreshed. Some of her play from there on in was of the utmost courage and fortitude. With her success, she would play Williams next, knowing that if she were to have any chance, she had to serve well from ➤

the outset and not lose her focus. Positivity, confidence and good thoughts. That was the way to do it.

Nikolay Davydenko, of Russia, said *dasvidania* at the first-round stage for the fifth time in his career as a largely unloved world No 4, whose life had been turned upside down in the past ten months because of a match he did not complete. Those who preferred their Russians to have graduated from the Marat Safin school of the slightly wild and menacing were not sorry to see the android-like baseliner bid farewell.

Davydenko lost 6-4 6-4 6-4 (even the score was dull) to Benjamin Becker of Germany. It was his 82nd match since one in Sopot, Poland, last August from which he retired hurt, something that looked, on the face of it, to be a harmless act, but was the signal for Betfair, the world's leading on-line betting exchange, to void bets that had reached a total of £3.5 million. Davydenko won the first set easily and yet, Martin Vassallo Arguello, an Argentinian ranked No.87 at the time, was still favoured to win in the Betfair market.

After almost every one of his subsequent matches, Davydenko has been asked if he knew of anything that he might have done wrong, about how he felt he had been treated and how it was affecting his life. He answered all inquiries as honestly as he could and, in the aftermath of his defeat to Becker, he shed more light on a dark corner of the sport.

He said he might have spoken a little to loudly to Irina, his wife, who was in the row behind him. "Maybe I could say something [like], 'I don't want to play,' or, 'I can retire,' " he said. "Some people can understand. It may be my mistake because I need to be quiet. I need to do only my job. I have tried to defend myself, but I have defended already for a year. I don't know how long I can defend myself. Maybe to the end of my career." One sincerely hoped not for Davydenko, deep down, is an honourable man.

Such assaults on one's integrity would have buried lesser men and the loss of a tennis match had come as little more than an aggravation to Davydenko by comparison with what he has described as "a bad dream, but not just for one day, but a few months". He was also asked – in jest it has to be said – if he was a betting man, who he would put his money on. He said probably Roger Federer or Rafael Nadal, "but I don't want to say about Andy Murray because you're Britain".

Nadal had opened his campaign with a 6-4 6-4 7-6 victory over German, Andreas Beck, a qualifier with a bludgeon of a serve but not enough to back it up with that caused the Spaniard too many problems. But better to get ➤

Andy Murray

this one out of the way without too much drawn from the energy reserves. "Today I served well," Nadal said. "Second record aces here. I had 18 two years ago against Agassi and today 17. So happy with my serve. I improve because I am young and I must improve. I practice for improve always. Every day, every month. My goal always is be better player, so for that reason I improved a little bit my serve."

And Andy Murray made an appearance, too. So much had been written on, speculated about and dreamed of for the British No.1 that it was just a relief to see him in the flesh, ready to play. His opponent was Fabrice Santoro, who had played 12 Wimbledons (having lost in the second round for the past six) and yet had never appeared on Centre Court in a singles match. This was to be the time and what an exhibition he provided, relishing the occasion hugely. He was aged 35 in his 64th grand-slam tournament, he knew

his way about and he has spent a career loving to tie up his opponents in a web of deceit. He and Murray played out a series of great points.

Murray mixed brilliance, inventiveness and touch with moments of total aberration. The torch, or baton that Tim Henman said was now the Scot's , has indeed been passed on. Santoro stretched Murray to a riveting tie-break in the third and final set, one that featured the Demented Drop Shot of the Day, and also a gloriously fortuitous net-cord winner. Nothing was ever safe, nothing was ever certain, the Centre Courters shouted their c'mons; the succession to Henman seemed assured.

It was farewell as a singles player to Jonas Bjorkman, the wonderful Swede, who had been a semi-finalist in 2006 when Federer was simply too good but was retiring to concentrate more on spending time with his young family. Bjorkman would be sorely missed, a gentleman of the game. He lost in four sets to Arnaud Clement, of France. *Hej Da* Jonas. ●

Day **THREE**
25.06.2008

DJOKOVIC
VS
SAFIN

IVANOVIC
VS
DECHY

FEDERER
VS
SÖDERLING

ZHENG JIE
VS
BALTACHA

S.WILLIAMS
VS
RADWANSKA

Spectators waiting to enter Wimbledon on the third day

Novak Djokovic

Wednesday June 25...

It had to happen. At the editorial gathering six months before The Championships to decide on the articles for the 2008 programme, the inevitable question came as to whether anyone had a special personality they particularly wanted to write about - a contender, a potential champion. Novak Djokovic's face immediately sprang to into one's head. On Day Three of the championships, the Serbian, who had subsequently won his first grand slam title at the Australian Open, taken the Pacific Life Open in Indian Wells, the Italian Open in Rome and had been to the finals of the Artois championships at Queen's Club (and was therefore living up to every expectation) was banished from the event. I don't know who took it harder.

Djokovic was beaten by Marat Safin, of Russia, actually not so much a defeat as a definitive spanking. Djokovic was simply a touch slow to everything all afternoon whereas Safin, a player who had said to me in April that he still believed he had one good grand slam left in him, played with a gilt-edged assurance. The Serb looked less than himself from the start and Safin took him out in straight sets, winning 6-4 7-6 6-2. At the start of every new game you expected the 21-year-old to find his range and blast the sabre-toothed Safin away. Failing that, you expected Safin to implode. Neither of these equally likely events took place.

Safin nailed the match the way he — sometimes — nails his ground strokes. "I took advantage that he was under a lot of pressure because he's fighting for No.1," the Russian said. Perhaps it was as simple as that. Djokovic's serve fell apart early, was mended, then fell apart again. It's a difficult transition to go from being a player for whom we have high hopes and to start being a player for whom we have high expectations and Djokovic failed to make it.

For the British, Djokovic's most important function had been as a stick for beating Andy Murray. They are the same age, they were more or less neck and neck in the race for the glittering prizes and, suddenly last summer, Djokovic surged ahead and did some achieving, while Murray, injury-struck, remained merely promising. Djokovic, though, played a callow match, while Safin kept it together admirably. Next time, Novak, next time. But he knew it, too, sending his PR manager a text which read "I've got a lot to learn."

At least Serbia survived the indignity of losing its two top draw attractions on the same afternoon, but it was mighty close. Ana Ivanovic, the new world No.1, arrived on grass not quite knowing what to expect. Chatting with her a couple of hours after her victory in the French Open at Roland Garros, her first grand slam triumph, she remarked on how difficult it was to transfer one's game in such a

Marat Safin

short space of time. She was not the first, nor would she be the last to feel that way.

"It is different, the points are so much faster, you have to be on the ball from the first point," she said. "I'm sure my fitness coach will be working on some specific movements because you can struggle with different muscle strains in the beginning." By comparison, Nathalie Dechy, of France, was a seasoned campaigner, a 29-year-old who was making this transition for the 13th time. Nothing ought to have come as a surprise to her. It was a real banana skin in the making for Ivanovic. Yet, the last time they had faced off in Amelia Island, Florida, the previous spring, Dechy did not have much fun. "I lost 6-1 6-1 and I didn't see the ball the whole match," she said. "I thought it was going to happen again. I am playing the No.1 player in the world on Court One and everything's going so fast. I had to do something." ➢

Nathalie Dechy

Ana Ivanovic

And so she did, extending Ivanovic to such an extent that had it not been for the flukiest net cord she will ever get, she would have been jostling with Djkovic for a first class seat on the first flight to Belgrade. Dechy had won the opening set having played a brutally efficient tie-break and led the second 5-4, on a second match point when Ivanovic's forehand - her best shot - clipped the top of the tape, appeared to want to make up its mind, and then tumbled gently in French territory. "I just thought the match was over," Ivanovic said. "The ball was in the air for a couple of seconds and I thought maybe it would go out." Ah well, we seasoned campaigners thought, that's it now.

But Dechy was made of sterner stuff, refusing to give ground in the third set, slugging it out point for excrutiating point, providing 18 of the most compelling games you could wish to see at Wimbledon but, eventually and sadly, Dechy cracked and lost 6-7 7-6 10-8. Ivanovic beamed, the French lady wept and said, through the tears: "Maybe somebody in the sky helped her."

Roger Federer required no such assistance from above. He was quickly wrapped back in his new fashion statement and, if his second-round victory over Robin Söderling, of Sweden, was not exactly a breeze, it continued to put the wind up those who have short memories as to the measure of his magnificence on grass.

Söderling, whose levels of commitment sometimes border on the downright antagonistic was beaten 6-3 6-4 7-6, and if the Swiss got a few steps wrong, he held enough sway to confirm his 61st consecutive victory on the surface. He lost his serve once, too, the first such indiscretion since the final of the French Open, but each time Söderling asked a question of him, the retort was immense. "I was on a similar streak when I didn't get broken from the Wimbledon quarter-finals of 2003, all the way to the quarters in '04," he said. "It was starting to get a burden because people were always reminding me about it." ➤

There is business to be done here and Federer looked as if he is in a mean mood. Söderling often had that effect on his opponents. They stiffened their sinews and dug a bit deeper because of the Swede's mannerisms - the way he shaped for his shots, his exaggerated fist-pumping when he won what would appear a rudimentary point - definitely buried under an opponent's skin. There was a moment in the second set when it looked as if he struck a ball hard at the world No.1. Federer had to turn his back and sway to one side in one move, which he managed to pull off as if troubled by a zephyr. One can think of a few players who might have glared, said a few choice words and one who might have dragged Söderling

Robin Söderling receives medical attention

up by his lapels, but Federer's response was simply to raise his levels and give his opponent a tennis lesson. And the match contained one of the sweetest shots of the fortnight, as Federer chased a lob, spun round, and contrived a forehand whipped across him that so stunned Söderling that he dumped his volley into the net.

Not many of us had taken a deal of notice of Zheng Jie of China up to this point. We knew that the contingent from that country was growing year on year, that she and Zi Yan had won the women's doubles title two years earlier and such was the interest and funding being ploughed into the game there, it would not be long before they became a truly significant force. ➤

Zheng Jie

Elena Baltacha

Zheng was playing Britain's Elena Baltacha in the second round, a couple of days after Baltacha's sobbing image had illuminated the pages of the British papers, as if sobbing and British tennis were inextricably linked. There were plenty of Kleenex being issued when Baltacha trailed 4-0 in the first set, almost before she had laid racket on ball. Zheng was a bundle of industry (much like her country), chasing, retrieving, knocking off winners.

Zheng completed a 6-2 7-5 victory but Baltacha was able to reflect on the fact that another year when nothing came easily to her might be the portent for that one when she can play, unfettered and without spending too much time in the doctor's waiting room, to kick her career on. "That (getting into the top 100 from the position of No.158 where she started the tournament) is definitely my main goal now. I've got the weapons, I just need to improve this consistency. My results are still a little bit all over the place, the way that I'm playing. So I really just need to knuckle down and just get that level, to maintain that level. But I think I've got the big shots and I think my serving needs to get better. My serve has been letting me down, as well. But I think it's exciting. I'm looking at it as a very positive experience, and I've still got a lot of things that can get better. And if I can improve it, then I think, yeah, I can break top 100."

Serena Williams did not have it all her own way against Urszula Radwanska, the younger of the two sisters from Poland and the previous year's girls champion (Agnieszka had won the same title in 2005). It took all of the former world No.1's gritty endeavour to emerge with a 6-4 6-4 victory and what she had seen of the little sister rather had her in mind of another rather famous tennis family. "I thought she was a really good opponent, I think she has a very bright future," Serena said. ●

Serena Williams

Urszula Radwanska

Day **FOUR**
26.06.2008

SHARAPOVA
VS
KUDRYAVTSEVA

RODDICK
VS
TIPSAREVIC

EATON
VS
TURSUNOV

NADAL
VS
GULBIS

MURRAY
VS
MALISSE

Alexander, Alla Kudryavtseva's father, celebrates his daughter's defeat of Maria Sharapova

Hands up all those who had a sneaking fancy for Maria Sharapova to land the ladies' championship and the next day be celebrating Andy Roddick's capture of the men's crown. The pair were not without their supporters and, after all, they both knew what it was like to win a grand slam (though not, in Roddick's case, the one he cherished above all). Instead, the interests of both were to be dealt an ignominious blow on a torrid Thursday.

Sharapova was beaten 6-2 6-4 by Alla Kudryavtseva, her fellow Russian, who went on to say that she just didn't like Sharapova's outfit and there was nothing left to do but to go out and give her a good smack. Which is exactly what she did. Roddick gave no offence to Janko Tipsarevic, of Serbia, save that his was a scalp worth having. The Centre Court offered him no means of protection – not even his own serve could do that – and a 6-7 7-5 6-4 7-6 defeat meant that he had lost at the second round stage of Wimbledon for the first time in his eight appearances.

Whether these would prove to be landmark losses, we would have plenty of time to find out but it was for certain that neither was expected. Kudryavtseva had been beaten in the first round of the Edgbaston Trophy in Birmingham two weeks earlier by Yorkshire's Katie O'Brien, a defeat that included a dreaded love set. Sharapova had chosen not to play on grass before The Championships, and her form at the French Open was pretty average, a first round victory over Evgeniya Rodina, 8-6 in the third and two further three set matches, the last of which was her fourth round defeat to Dinara Safina.

For all her complicated traversing of the world – which included a Fed Cup appearance in Israel just to complicate matters – Sharapova had won just two titles, in Doha and Amelia Island. Her 2008 form was sketchy to say the least. And when she walked out on No.1 court, something overcame her opponent which was to have a powerful effect.

There were so many fashion statements being made this year it was hard to know where to start, Roger Federer's woolly, Serena Williams' mackintosh and then there were Sharapova's short shorts. To the untrained eye, they looked rather smart but obviously what is nothing to get into a state about for a middle-aged writer, becomes something that provokes a degree of agitation in 20-year-old female tennis players.

Perhaps Sharapova should have been warned. After all, Kudryavtseva's father, Alexander, was a world champion wrestler and she owns a rottweiler named Ralph. When it comes to fighting spirit, Sharapova ➢

Alla Kudryavtseva

Maria Sharapova

could have guessed that her opponent was up for a heck of a tennis match, as indeed it proved. But there was worse to come, for Kudryavtseva, not one of the glamour girls of tennis, said that Sharapova's status as a fashion icon had got under her skin. "It's very pleasant to beat Maria," she said. "I don't like her outfit. Can I put it this way? It was one of my motivations to beat her."

My, Kudryavtseva must have bristled when she set eyes on her opponent. As always, Sharapova looked wonderful: trim, athletic and shrieking for Russia as she boomed the ball around the court. That was part of the problem, for Sharapova boomed the ball almost anywhere but where it was supposed to go. As the second round wore on, the 2004 champion looked as though she was trying to take on the worries of the world, alternating between huge bursts of energy and tired, listless shots with all the power of a powder puff. At least she was gracious in the face of a humbling defeat.

"I guess it wasn't my day," Sharapova said. "She just did everything better than I did. She played much better, she had nothing to lose, she went for her shots. I was pretty tentative.

You just never know what's going to happen on any given day. Some days the balls just don't bounce where you want them or they don't land where you want them to land."
L. Jon Wertheim, writing in the legendary American magazine *Sports Illustrated*, remarked: "It's no coincidence that Sharapova blew off the grasscourt tune-ups and was so flat here. She clearly intended to use the early rounds as practice, but you can't do that any more in the women's game. This field is deep and the first week is no longer a cakewalk. The WTA's marketing machine got a flat tyre this week. But if no other good comes of results like this, I suspect the field for the 2009 Eastbourne tune-up event will be radically improved."

Roddick knew how she felt. When a player who needs every bit of his serving armoury to be firing, the interruption to the American's season when he tweaked something in the nape of his neck in Rome, had dramatic effects. He missed the French Open and arrived at Queen's far too uncooked. He lost there to Rafael Nadal and did not play another competitive match before The Championships.

Janko Tipsarevic

Andy Roddick

Chris Eaton

He was meat and drink for a player like Janko Tipsarevic, an indomitable Serb, who hustles and bustles around the court, finding shots where none should be found, making the kind of improvised winners that eventually tired Roddick down. The American was simply not into his game enough to react. If there were awards for candour, Roddick would have won many trophies by now – no one wore their heart any bigger on their sleeve. No one hurt more deeply when they lost, especially at Wimbledon. For all the self-delusion in sport, Roddick knows exactly what the reality of his situation is, both micro ('I choked by playing two of the worst shots ever') and macro ('it's all about winning another slam.') Really, his session was exceptional in its honest self-assessment.

Here are a couple of gems. "I was literally trying to make him play. I thought he was pretty tight also. That's not the way – you just got to reverse the mentality of putting it in and hoping he's going to miss. I just didn't make anything happen out there tonight. Zero, zero, zero." He followed that with: "I played just horrific shots on breakpoints both ways. He was a hundred percent on breakpoints, I was 0 for 58. I put myself in position to win that match in straight sets. I served huge tonight and I actually returned well in spots. It's not the same as '06 where I couldn't have hit the ball into an ocean from the beach. It was just the big moments. I blinked. You know, there's no way of getting around that."

Chris Eaton's fine run came to an end as one might have expected against Dmitry Tursunov, a Russian who has been good enough to reach the top 20 two years ago but had shaved off his carroty beard, which made him look all the more leaner and meaner. Tursuno won 7-6 6-2 6-4, to bring the Surrey player's bit of fun to an end. Eaton learned a lot about himself, his tennis and what more can come from him. The inimitable Simon Barnes, in *The Times* rose to his occasion, too.

"He is a big lad and still walks with a kind of amiable oafish teenager slouch, as if he is not quite at home yet in his prodigious body. But he gives the ball a fair old tap and seems to like it when an entire nation is looking at him — never a bad thing for a tennis player. He is a good-looking lad, in a dark and bristly, bulky sort of way — certainly anyone who thought otherwise was in a minority. Chris! Chris! Oh Chris!

"So let us not dwell on the callow errors, the trying-too-hard groundstrokes that went wildly long, the vulnerability to the wiliness and movement of his opponent. Let us rather cheer for the good bits: a great worm-killer of a serve and a love of the volley, great lunging put-aways, a general love of lording it at the ➤

Rafael Nadal

net and daring his opponent to try to get past. He is aware that he can be an intimidating sight and did his best to chivvy and bully an opponent who has seen most things but has not often met a hulking serve-and-volleying sex god in front of his own people and all flush with the excitement of sudden fame."

Back in the real world, Ernests Gulbis was reminding us again that he is a top ten player in the making. The 19-year-old Latvian took the first set off Rafael Nadal on No.1 court; indeed we were seven games into the match before Nadal took even so much as a point off Gulbis' serve. It was clear, from early on, that the slightest advance either player could make on the other's service game would need to be capitalised on. And so it was all the more agonising for Nadal that, at 30-all and chasing a game that would have given him the chance to serve for the first set, he was on the end of a shocking 'not up' call while dashing to retrieve one of Gulbis' artful drop shots. Nadal exploded with anger, lost the game and found himself facing set point after a superb lob.

As Nadal sets himself to serve, there is a closely observed concentration gathering ritual during which there will be at least five bounces of the ball off the racket and then between five and ten bounces out of the hand. Reflecting the additional tension of the moment, on this occasion there were nine bounces off the racket and 13 out of the hand — a European record (or so it was claimed!). Gulbis took the point, nevertheless, and Nadal was in the unusual position of being a set behind in the early stages of a tournament.

Unfortunately, Gulbis could carry the momentum he had gained only a short distance into the second set. With Nadal misfiring, and marginally distracted, the Latvian might have moved decisively ahead in the second game but Nadal hung on and then broke in the third and again in the fifth. It was not until the third set that Gulbis again found the opportunity to impose himself to the extent that he had in the first. He matched Nadal for its duration and the Spaniard needed a tie-break to extend his lead.

Even in the fourth set, which Nadal won with a single break in the eighth game, Gulbis was always in touch, nervelessly so. When Gulbis could go in hard and get the job done quickly, he prospered, though most rallies of any duration were won by Nadal and, in the end, it was his speed around the place, allied to his belligerent levels of tenacity, that separated him from an opponent who will go far.

Oh, and Andy Murray reached the third round with a straight set win over Xavier Malisse of Belgium. He was serving brilliantly and performing well within himself. This was getting really interesting. ●

Guillermo Garcia-Lopez

MATCH of the Day
GUILLERMO GARCIA-LOPEZ (SPAIN)
BEAT NICOLAS ALMAGRO (SPAIN)
6-3 3-6 5-7 6-1 6-2

Garcia-Lopez had won two matches in his Wimbledon career, Almagro, the No.19 seed, who ended Murray's hopes in a wondrous match at the French Open four weeks earlier, had not won a round before, having been beaten by Dmitry Tursunov (twice) and Mario Ancic. Yet these two produced a brilliant match, rally upon rally of intense concentration and application. From two sets to one up, one would have thought that Almagro, one of the players of the year, would march on but Garcia-Lopez prevailed. Spain's mistrust of grass was well and truly over.

ANCIC
VS
FERRER

MATTEK
VS
BARTOLI

MAURESMO
VS
S. WILLLIAMS

ZHENG
VS
IVANOVIC

VAIDISOVA
VS
DELLACQUA

REYNOLDS
VS
VERDASCO

Mario Ancic

Friday 27 June…

It was not as if it was a unique gesture, people had been kissing the Centre Court grass (and nobbling bits of it and shoving them in their racket bags in Martina Navratilova's case) for some years now. Bjorn Borg did it at the Champions' Parade in 2000, the first time he had returned to Wimbledon since his final match at The Championships in 1981. Funny that now we could not keep the Swede away from the premises.

When Mario Ancic knelt and gave the turf a smacker after his third round victory over David Ferrer, the No.5 seed from Spain, three hours and 11 minutes of splendidly gruelling tennis completed in semi-darkness, there was a touch more than the oft-believed 'I love this place and this place loves me' sentiment. Ancic had been waiting for this moment for the best part of 18 months and had wondered if it would ever happen for him.

Every once in a while something comes along that interrupts the beauty of everyday life and what had been taken for granted is to be cherished, sought after, dreamt about. One recalled shaking Ancic's hand at Wimbledon last September – he walked over and proffered his, which shows what a well-bred man he is – during the Davis Cup World Group qualifier between Great Britain and Croatia and saying how glad I was to see him. Never more so.

He was merely practising, his green shirt dripping sweat and, although not fit enough to play in the tie, he had wanted to feel the grass beneath his feet one more time. Six months earlier, it was all he could do to climb out of bed and, after 15 minutes walking like an elderly gentleman on Eastbourne promenade, he had to lie down again. Often he spent 18 hours a day in a darkened room, sipping soup and eating minute salad portions. Ancic was the victim of a bout of glandular fever so virulent that he wondered if he would play sport professionally again.

Briefly, having played a Davis Cup match in Germany, Ancic woke unable to swallow or eat and was coughing up blood. "I had never felt as bad as I did there," he said. The doctors diagnosed a severe case of flu, so Ancic flew to the next tournament in Marseilles, where, after the first four games of his first-round match, he could not move. "I had a huge fever, I don't know how I got home to Croatia and they diagnosed me pretty quickly," Ancic said. "I remember that it was a beautiful weekend, I wanted to walk on the beach, but after 15 minutes my legs gave out. My liver was completely gone, the enzyme count was rocketing – in the sky. I lost so much weight and my muscles were reduced because, if you don't train for ten days, you start to lose muscle mass. I lost everything."

Mario Ancic

Remarkable that he had found it all again, enough to have taken his place at the tennis shrine – a court he called 'this holy place' – and when he completed a bravura 6-4 6-4 6-7 7-6 victory over Ferrer, the Duracell Bunny of the men's tour, it was tantamount to taking The Championship itself. We felt as good for him as Ancic felt for himself.

Asked about the puckering up, he said: "It was a flashback from everything what was going on in my head, what was going on in the year that I was not able to play. It was almost like saying – here I am back again. Thanks. I love this court at Wimbledon. It means so much to me."

It was a heck of an effort to win, too, because every point against Ferrer had to be gained at maximum output, he did not relent, he kept coming back for more, he was Rafael Nadal without the personality. Perhaps, one day, that would come as well and watch him go then. Ancic was rightly beside himself with the significance of the win and where it occured.

Croatia may have been loving it, but the French were having a *mauvais* day. It wasn't much fun being an American male player either – of which more later. Marion Bartoli, the surprise women's runner-up in 2007, was beaten in straight sets by Bethanie Mattek, a Minnesotan with plenty of get up and go who did not know the meaning of the phrase 'backward step'. Bartoli, who had maintained enough of last summer's form to have entered The Championships as the No.11 seed put it down to not having a good day and a stiff shoulder which she said had been exacerbated by a sudden dip in temperatures midway through the afternoon. Mattek, naturally, begged to differ.

She confessed that, in the past, her career had been shaped more by the clothes she wore than the matches she won. (Remember the long socks on Centre Court a couple of years back?). Now at No.69 in the world, things were progressing in her game as well. "It's not that I didn't take my career serious, or even myself," she said. "I'm still outgoing and like to show my personality. But I really wanted to have my tennis come through. That's why I've kind of toned down some of my outfits for this tournament. I get players coming up to me and they're all disappointed in me. I'm like, Guys! I still have a bunch of outfits. I have a clothing sponsor now. It's just for right now I'm focusing on my tennis." And doing a pretty decent job of it.

Bethanie Mattek

Serena Williams

Marat Safin

Amelie Mauresmo's bid to play the second week of a grand slam for the first time in a year, also foundered. Not unexpectedly. Of all the players to face when you are not sure where you game is, or even if you *really* want to be out there, it is Serena Williams. Mauresmo, the 2006 champion, lost 7-6 6-1. There had been physical problems, demoralising ones for her, and that did not help her general demeanour.

"I have a lot of respect for Mauresmo," Williams said, "I guess she just had her appendix removed not too long ago. I think she's playing unbelievable tennis. To win Wimbledon at any point is the highlight of one's career. I love playing her. We always have a good match. She has a very different game, a very different style. I think we bring our best tennis with each other." But such was the one-sidedness of the outcome, Williams found herself having to fend off questions which ranged in the disbelief stakes from which of the American presidential candidates, Senator McCain or Senator Obama she would prefer to present the US Open trophy should she win it in September; to the make-up of her ideal man; to her thoughts about the Taj Majal. Funny, I thought this was supposed to be a tennis tournament. ➤

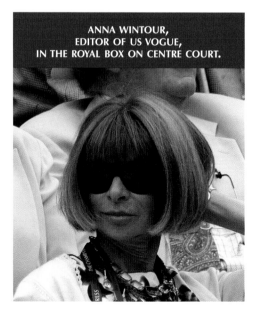

ANNA WINTOUR,
EDITOR OF US VOGUE,
IN THE ROYAL BOX ON CENTRE COURT.

Zheng Jie

No-one asked Ana Ivanovic about the Taj Majal which is just as well – most of us were worried more about her third round defeat to Zheng Jie, of China. It is not as if we had not seen it coming, Zheng had taken her to three sets in their only previous meeting in Montreal two years earlier, Ivanovic had escaped by the skin of her teeth in the second round and had not looked entirely comfortable at all. The result was a thoroughly creditable 6-1 6-4 victory for the Chinese wild card.

Zheng was smaller and more agile, Ivanovic found bending and striking balls which stayed low a touch too demanding. She had no complaints but put some of this setback down to the emotional strain of winning the French Open and reaching the No.1 ranking in the world in one fell, remarkable swoop. She would come back a stronger, more resilient performer.

Ana Ivanovic

We had hoped the same would happen for Nicola Vaidisova. The engaging blonde from the Czech Republic, who had progressed in the past three years at Wimbledon from third round, to fourth, to quarter-final, had been having a terrible year, her motivation waning, her shots straying, her concentration wavering. She had chosen to turn to David Felgate, Tim Henman's coach for nine years, in an effort to turn things around, only to suffer an abysmal clay court run which made Felgate wonder if he had done the right thing.

Now, Vaidisova was showing the urgency Felgate demanded, the feel was coming back into her strokes, the ability to use her strengths – standing at 6'1" afforded her certain advantages – and a 6-2 6-4 victory over Casey Dellacqua, the tough Australian left-hander, was obvious evidence of rejuvenation. "David brings a different approach than I've been used to. He's a very positive guy, very patient. It's just exciting to do it a little differently. It's a good challenge for both of us. I'm very excited about it."

There was one American male player in the third round. Roddick? No. Blake? No. Spadea? No. Young? No. Step forward and take the acclaim one Bobby Reynolds, ranked No.102 who was doing his thing with some purpose, though it was to come to an end against Fernando Verdasco, the talented Spaniard. It reminded one that Pete Sampras had just completed his book – *A Champion's Mind*, in collaboration with the excellent Peter Bodo. The seven times Wimbledon champion, who had not returned since his final Championship, in 2002, was a marvel to work with, Bodo discovered. "Sampras showed a remarkable facility for cutting to the chase – for 'keeping it real'," the author said. "He wanted *A Champion's Mind* to be a tennis memoir, the book his grandchildren would read if they were curious about him. He had no interest in settling scores or satisfying voyeuristic urges regarding those aspects of his personal life that had no real bearing on his career. He wanted to be honest and revealing, but only about things that really mattered.

"These aspirations may seem humble and perhaps even quaint in today's supercharged market for tell-all, confessional, revisionist autobiographies. But Sampras is Sampras, ever true to himself. Sampras was able to tell me how he felt about almost anything in the proverbial 500 words or fewer. We had no lengthy candlelit dinners after which, loaded on red wine, he broke down and talked for four hours about how he really feels about his father."

We had missed Sampras across the years and hoped that he would come back home one day. ●

Nicola Vaidisova

Day **SIX**
28.06.2008

JANKOVIC
vs
WOZNIACKI

MURRAY
vs
HAAS

NADAL
vs
KIEFER

V. WILLIAMS
vs
MARTINEZ SANCHEZ

Jelena Jankovic

Saturday 28 June…

The middle Saturday of each Championships had become a jamboree, with the prospect of bumping into a living sporting legend each time you turned a corner. Sir Geoff Hurst and I almost walked straight into each other and that is worth cherishing because even after 42 years mourning a national football team that cannot win anything, greeting the hat-trick hero of 1966 warmed the cockles. It is 72 years since the British celebrated a male champion in SW19 but let's not go there.

The Royal Box was top heavy with superstars from so many sports, all of whom one wished it were possible to spend a few minutes in the company of; Sir Geoff, Sir Bobby Charlton; Sir Bobby Robson from football, Lord Sebastian Coe, Dame Kelly Holmes, Sir Steve Redgrave and Matthew Pinsent, noble Olympians all, and young Danny Cipriani, who could become a real star in rugby union. There was space for the non-

Caroline Wozniacki

athletes too and one doubted there had been, or would be, a pinker tie the entire fortnight than that adorning Sir Terry Wogan.

This day, a year ago, and the dignitaries were draped in blankets (galoshes and duffel coats would have been useful extras) and saw just about an hour's play. This time the sun continued to dazzle, there had been only a couple of brief interruptions for rain in the opening week and the tournament was right on schedule. Oh happy, happy days.

What Centre Court fare for them, too – matches involving Jelena Jankovic, the top seed remaining in the ladies' singles, Andy Murray, the only British player in any main draw singles and Rafael Nadal whose stealthy pursuit of Roger Federer promised an enthralling climax to the men's singles.

Jankovic was hardly her usual life and soul. It had not been one of Serbia's finer weeks what with Novak Djokovic and Ana Ivanovic tumbling out before they had got their knees dirty and fears of a wipe-out of their favourites duly surfaced. Jankovic's left knee was being swathed in bandages as her third-round match with 17-year-old Caroline Wozniacki, of Denmark – a real prospect – stood at one set all. After two more changes of end, the trainer came back, the last visit to have all said strapping removed, because Jankovic found her movement terribly restricted. "The knee was getting numb" she said. "There was just even more pain." Apparently, the trainer was not exactly chuffed at having to undo all the good work she had done – "but I was taking a risk to get injured more, but that is what I chose because I wanted to win," the player said in mitigation.

Although Jankovic, with the tiniest of squeals, revealed something was amiss with her leg as early as the third game, it was the court craft of the Dane that gave her more problems. What all this was doing to the concentration of an inexperienced teenager is open to speculation, but Wozniacki conceded her serve three times in the final set and succumbed, 2-6 6-4 6-2.

Off limped Jankovic, happy to be 'alive' still, to be replaced by the sprightly Andy Murray. What a welcome he received for a third round meeting with Tommy Haas, the experienced German who could have told Jankovic a thing or ten about how to smile in the face of physical adversity. What he didn't know about injuries was barely worth knowing.

Up against him was a British No.1 in the rudest of health. Apart from having to withdraw from the Artois championships at Queen's Club, nine days before this tournament, with a thumb injury, Murray had been in buoyant form since the French Open, ➤

Sir Bobby Charlton, Sir Bobby Robson, Sir Matthew Pinsent, Sir Steve Redgrave and Martina Navratilova were among the Royal Box guests

Judy Murray

far more mellow, eager to engage, helpful and, as ever, a fount of good quotable material. He mentioned that he had recently acquired a border terrier puppy for Kim Sears, his girlfriend, and they had decided to call it Maggie, after Maggie May, the Rod Stewart stalwart. Maggie was commissioned to write a diary by *The Times*.

Tuesday: "I watched the Master prepare himself for his opening game. 'If you want my body, and you think I'm sexy, come on sugar let me know,' he sang and I woofed along in harmony. That's how I got found out by security." "Out," a burly man in uniform said. "There's only one barker allowed in here and that's Sue."

Thursday: "I've almost forgiven the Master for telling the media about my toilet problem. I'd like to see him maintain bladder control when watching Maria Sharapova try to hold serve. Andy sat down with Mother Judy to work out a strategy for his third-round match with a German. 'I need to be properly Haas-trained,' the Master said. You and me both, Andy." All wonderful knockabout stuff.

The match against Haas was everything Murray could have expected it to be, if not a walk in the park, because he dropped his first set of The Championships. His unruffled manner was underlined when the experienced German snatched the momentum at the end of the second set that would, in the past, have provoked, at least, a noisy bout of self-derision and quite possibly a concentration-shattering tantrum.   ➤

Tommy Haas

**Looking on.
Sue Barker, Tim Henman
and John McEnroe.**

Not this time, however, as the Scot displayed the calm that showed his new-found maturity and quietly regrouped, took a moment or two to assess the situation and coolly reasserted his early dominance to grind out any hope that might have been growing across the net. There was much to savour from Murray, his service continued to have plenty of pep, he was quicker and more fluent around the court, his backhand down the line continued to ooze class and, quite frankly, there was a buzz about him here that had not been noted before. Summing up his new outlook at the close of a 6-4 6-7 6-3 6-2 victory, which ensured a fourth round meeting with Richard Gasquet of France, he declared: "I'm enjoying myself when I'm on the court now rather than it being a bit of a drag."

He knew, only too well, that he squandered the chance of a third successive straight-sets victory by allowing his standard to drop momentarily in the second set tie-break. Wisely, he did not allow such a change of fortune to lead to a crisis. "I stayed focused on the next set and mentally my approach was good," said the 12th seed, who lost to Haas in their previous meeting in Indian Wells, California in March because he had allowed

Nicolas Kiefer

his focus to dip. "Now I have got to keep this up. The older you get, the more you get used to everything. In the past I struggled to deal with situations and in a couple more years I will be playing my best tennis. I'm going to have to play better if I want to go further."

Which brought on Nadal against another German, Nicolas Kiefer, who had been around the game a long time but had never quite shaken its foundations. In hindsight, Kiefer had one chance to put pressure on the No.2 seed. One point, in fact, which came in the eighth game of the opening set. It came out of the blue, as Nadal went from the ➤

security of a 40-0 lead to deuce, the German benefiting from a rare double-fault and a beautifully constructed point as Kiefer put away a volley into an open court after pulling his opponent wide on the forehand.

A break point to Kiefer, the pressure momentarily on the favourite. Enter the real Nadal, the Nadal who has noticed the look in the eye of Tiger Woods at moments of real pressure and likes what he sees. Like Andre Agassi, who used to surprise opponents on critical points by serving and volleying, Nadal swung his first serve wide and hustled to the net to sweep away the volley. For Kiefer, that was pretty well his only glimpse of a future, for he then realised, all too clearly, the true balance of Centre Court power. The crowd, soporific in the encroaching shadow, sensed the significance of the tie-break, certainly for the underdog, yet it was no contest. Kiefer's serve, so reliable for an hour, fell horribly to pieces, Nadal moved to a new gear and the No.27 seed's desperation was betrayed in the two unforced errors that ultimately cost him the tie-break 7-3 and, with almost indecent haste, the match, 7-6 6-2 6-3.

Venus Williams, the champion, found herself on Court No.1 against Maria Jose Martinez Sanchez, a 25-year-old Spaniard ranked No.101 who had not figured on many radars before this engagement. Williams ended both sets of her 6-1 7-5 victory with an ace, the second timed at 127mph, not just an emphatic conclusion to the match but also a Wimbledon best. Venus had equalled her sister's record of 126mph last year but with this fire-cracker, she had edged to within two mph of her own world record, set last year in the US Open.

As the speed guns are a little suspect, this says nothing other than Venus is beginning to find her rhythm after a season interrupted by injury and loss of confidence. Like Pete Sampras before her, though, she delighted in becoming a Wimbledon specialist, peaking for the one tournament she believed was her birthright. It was difficult to tell the exact state of the champion's game for the strapping Spaniard took 23 minutes to cast off her understandable nerves, forfeiting the first five games in 17 minutes, and journeying deep into the second set before she really began to mount some resistance.

Whatever the Spanish term for journeyman is, it applied to Martinez Sanchez, who had the misfortune to have not one, but two, grand slam champions in her surname. She was a decent doubles player and a series of acute angled backhand volleys and one sweet stop-volley, feathered over the net as Williams was rooted to the baseline, showed a touch of real class. A rout was turned, however briefly, into a contest.

From 2-4 down in the second set, Martinez Sanchez broke back to lead 5-4, giving a passable imitation of Manuel Santana, albeit female and left-handed (but how many other Spanish serve-and-volleyers can you remember?) The crowd responded with understandable fervour, no reflection of their indifference to Williams, just an appreciation of the Spaniard's belated bravado. That is all it amounted to, however. ●

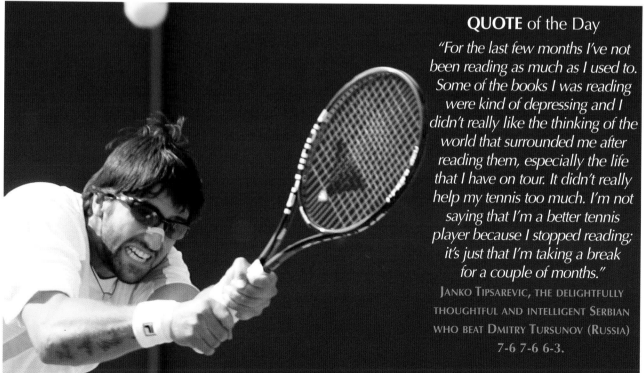

QUOTE of the Day

"For the last few months I've not been reading as much as I used to. Some of the books I was reading were kind of depressing and I didn't really like the thinking of the world that surrounded me after reading them, especially the life that I have on tour. It didn't really help my tennis too much. I'm not saying that I'm a better tennis player because I stopped reading; it's just that I'm taking a break for a couple of months."

JANKO TIPSAREVIC, THE DELIGHTFULLY THOUGHTFUL AND INTELLIGENT SERBIAN WHO BEAT DMITRY TURSUNOV (RUSSIA) 7-6 7-6 6-3.

Day **SEVEN**
30.06.2008

Monday 30 June...

There were so many wonderful matches, so much to savour, so many opportunities to get within touching distance of the best players in the world and so few clouds in the sky. Was there a day in grand slam tennis quite like a sunny second Monday when the round of 16 was to be completed? There were to be 26 interviews conducted in the main room alone so more than a word of praise was merited for Jamie Morrocco and Julie Rabe, the steadfast stenographers.

While their fingers did the walking to keep up with the superstars talking, so it was difficult for us chroniclers to know where to turn next. The Williams sisters, with six singles titles for family heirlooms, were both given

No.2 court dates and were scheduled to play their doubles there too. They tried to grin and bear it. Jelena Jankovic, seeded No.2, was not happy in the slightest to find herself and Tamarine Tanasugarn of Thailand walking onto Court No.18, a pretty enough venue, tucked in the corner by the Broadcast Centre, but not quite what she had been expecting. A complaint went in to Larry Scott, the CEO of the Sony Ericsson WTA Tour.

"I've spoken to Venus, Serena and Jelena and they're quite pleased I'm going to be taking this up directly with the chairman," Scott said. "I was disappointed and concerned and share the concern of our players. I've committed to them that I would take this up this week." Though he did not want to make this an overt man v. woman confrontation, when it was pointed out that Roger Federer, Rafael Nadal and Andy Murray had played all their matches on the two main courts (indeed Murray, the 12th seed, had been scheduled on Centre in each of his four matches) he added: "That speaks for itself."

Wimbledon's referee, Andrew Jarrett – forever the diplomat – countered that organising the packed schedule meant not all players could appear on the courts they preferred. "With 16 matches to play on six show courts, it is inevitable that some leading players will be scheduled away from Centre and No.1," he said. "This is always the case on the second Monday at Wimbledon and as such provides a great opportunity for spectators." How to disarm in 44 words.

Well, almost disarm. Serena was spitting feathers, even though her 6-3 6-3 victory over Bethanie Mattek, a fellow American, was as routine as these things ever are. "Initially I thought, 'is this the right schedule?' I thought maybe there was a mistake," Serena said upon discovering she and Venus had been left off the two main show courts – or 'dissed', to use the language of their home town, Los Angeles. "I haven't seen Roger Federer on No.2 Court in, like, six years," Serena added. "I think it is weird, especially having a female champ (in Venus) who has won this tournament four times."

Still, no matter, the dimensions of the court do not vary once one steps outside where you do feel cut off from the rest of The Championship. Soon after Serena had ambled through, Venus completed a 6-3 6-4 victory over Alisa Kleybanova, the Russian teenager, who put up a fight only when it was far too late. As had been her wont, Venus used the opening round, or two, to find her range and, with Kleybanova struggling to land a first serve in the London Borough of Merton, she had only to raise her game a touch to see off the Russian's late rally. ➤

Venus Williams

83

There was a scramble for the record books when the clearly ailing Jankovic lost to Tanasugarn and joined Ana Ivanovic and Maria Sharapova on the route march home, the first time since records began that the top three seeds have failed to reach the quarter-finals of a grand slam tournament. Jankovic did not depart without adding her complaints about the schedule, both on behalf of herself, stuck out on No.18 Court, and for Venus. "It was not right," she said. "I don't know what they are doing to put Venus on No.2 and I'm on 18. I was almost playing in the parking lot. I almost needed a helicopter."

No one reminded Jankovic that had she been on one of the two major courts and been as hurt as she undoubtedly was, the reaction to her 6-3 6-2 defeat may have been a good deal more shrill. As it was, she could pack her bags and scarper (well, limp) almost unnoticed.

**Above: Tamarine Tanasugarn
Left: Jelena Jankovic**

Andy Murray could not have left the grounds in a mood further removed from that of Jankovic. It pitch black by that time but there was a palpable sense of light at the end of the tunnel. Murray had beaten Richard Gasquet to reach the quarter-finals of a grand slam tournament for a first time; well, it was not so much a victory as a renaissance, a discovery, a real moment.

Gasquet, at one point, was serving for the match. It would have been a straight-sets victory and it would have been well merited; a player who, at all stages, had seemed ever so slightly stronger, and in grass-court tennis little things go a very long way. How did it turn around? Was it the crowd that lifted Murray? Was it Murray's desperate defiance that inspired the crowd to play their best game? ➤

Andy Murray

The result was a glorious symbiosis and the two partners gave us one of the great tea-time excesses that have been part of the British summer since Tim Henman first found that a British player on Centre Court finds things within himself unobtainable elsewhere. A remarkable match ended 5-7 3-6 7-6 6-2 6-4 in Murray's favour and, with this result, the Scot has truly arrived as a top-quality player. He showed fight and passion – and at the end, an impossible coolness – and thoroughly deserved his victory in a genuine Wimbledon epic.

It came down to the minutest differentials. And there really were not all that many; Gasquet, at 22, a year older and, at No.10, one place higher in the world rankings. Both are talented ball players, ambitious, eager and at times breathtaking to watch. They can both construct fabulous points, both can turn defence into attack with a sudden twist of the imagination. Right from the first, this looked like a good one.

They were toe to toe in the first set, 11 games, no breaks and just as we were composing ourselves for the tie-break, the smallest, tiniest thing went amiss, and made all the difference. Murray made a couple of ground-stroke errors to trail 15-30, he missed his first serve and then put the second into the net at 69mph. It was an attack of the yips, nothing less. So there was the first set, there was the momentum and there was Murray struggling. The manner in which a player struggles is deeply indicative of his nature and Murray believes that, when in doubt, you go to the drop shot. As a point of information, when Murray is not in doubt it is because he has already played a drop shot.

So when he served for the first time in the second set, two successive muffed drop shots opened the way and then a wince-making double fault handed Gasquet a break point. As a result, he took the game and then the set.

A couple of bad points, that's all it took; a couple of bad serves. Why should the second serve break down at these points of all points? Work it out for yourself. It looked all over, it really did.

Gasquet served for the match and that is when Murray's extraordinary revival began. The signs were there that he had been relishing the struggle and soon he began to thrive on it. Murray and the crowd got working and together they put the worm of doubt into Gasquet's mind. From then on, it was glorious stuff, the stuff that brings us back to this tournament year after year; Murray came back from a break down to win a sensational tie-break, winning a decisive rally despite playing a drop shot that did not work out and sealing it with a running backhand that darn near took him head first into the photographers' pit. It was wild stuff of pure inspiration, crowd and player sharing the same frenzy. If Murray had played naked and covered in woad, he could hardly have given a more atavistic performance.

And then another mood swing; Murray calm, Murray in control, Murray going a break up. Gasquet looked rattled; a man he had more or less beaten was now outplaying him. Murray took the fourth set, with a double break, and we were off into the fifth. The light began to fade, but the tennis did not. Every point was played as if lives were dependent upon it, both players coming up with points that you simply should not play in a normal state of consciousness.

As Simon Barnes said in *The Times* "Murray, stone blind in the glorious nature of sport, somehow stormed off a service break in the first game, flirted with a break on his own serve and then, with a magnificent reassertion of his own will, managed to cling on. It was now Murray's to lose as the sun went down, finding aces, relishing the new revelation of himself to himself. For the first time, he looked like a man of destiny." ➤

Richard Gasquet

Mario Ancic

If one has perhaps over-sold the Murray match as opposed to reflecting more on others, it is because it was the match that made the day. And yet there were many more than he that day who did wondrous things. Mario Ancic, for instance, defeated Fernando Verdasco, the Spanish left hander, 3-6 3-6 6-3 6-4 13-11, a match than enthralled No.11 Court for the best part of five hours. Verdasco had led by two sets to one, 4-2 and thirty-love; here was Ancic living up to all that he had promised. The engaging Croat was into the last eight.

Feliciano Lopez was there, too, another left handed Spaniard who tended to show all of his many virtues at this time of year. Lopez, you will recall, was the man who brought the curtain down on Tim Henman's Wimbledon career a year earlier, and here he was, dusting the event with his magic again, a five set victor over Marcos Baghdatis, of Cyprus, 8-6 in the fifth.

A former champion, indeed the last men's champion before Roger Federer, was beaten in straight sets – Lleyton Hewitt, of Australia, was vanquished by Federer himself so there was some symmetry there. Any hope of an all Swiss men's final was banished when Stanislas Wawrinka, who had entered the top ten for the first time in May when he reached the final of the Rome Masters, was beaten in four sets by the rejuvenated Marat Safin.

The sound of seeds with crushed egos in the women's event had not ceased. Svetlana Kuznetsova, the No.4 seed, was beaten in three sets by the composed Pole, Agnieszka Radwanska; Anna Chakvetadze, the No.8 seed, fell to Nicole Vaidisova, of the Czech Republic and the No.15 seed, Agnes Szavay, of Hungary, was downed in straight sets by Zheng Jie, of China. What a tale was beginning to unfold there. ●

QUOTE of the Day

JUSTINE HENIN THE WORLD NO.1 WHO RETIRED SIX WEEKS EARLIER, SPEAKING FROM LIMELETTE, BELGIUM WHERE SHE WAS NOW RUNNING A TENNIS ACADEMY:

"I know Wimbledon is going on and I'm following the results a little bit but, for me, it seems so far away. I don't need the adrenalin of being in front of 20,000 people any more. I need intensity in my life but it comes from different things now."

Lleyton Hewitt

Roger Federer and Lleyton Hewitt

Day **EIGHT**
1.07.2008

MURRAY AND HUBER
VS
KNOWLE AND CHAN

V. WILLIAMS
VS
TANASUGARN

ZHENG JIE
VS
VAIDISOVA

S. WILLIAMS
VS
RADWANSKA

Tuesday 1 July…

The lasting image of the previous evening had been Andy Murray flexing his right bicep. It was meant, he said, not as a challenge to Rafael Nadal but an indication that the work he had been putting in with his fitness team had begun to pay Ramboesque dividends. Those scrawny individuals among us chose to wear long-sleeved shirts on Tuesday, even though it was warm enough to fry an egg on St Mary's Walk.

Manic Monday had given way to Tender Tuesday, the women's quarter-finals that were not anywhere near the matches we had anticipated when the draw was made. Each of the matches had a rich promise, each demanded some of one's time, but it was an opportunity to spread the wings and search for riches on the outside courts where, after the previous day's shenanigans, the committee had chosen not to put any of the women's last eight.

**Liezel Huber and
Jamie Murray**

We had reached the second round stage of the junior championships – Bernard Tomic, the 15-year-old Australian who had won his home Open and reached the quarter-finals in Roland Garros, was beginning to get his Wimbledon career underway on Court No.19, dropping the first set to the only Indonesian male in any of the competitions, Christopher Rungkat, but recovering to win in three; Grigor Dimitrov, likewise the lone male Bulgarian in The Championships, had a tough first round against Britain's Niall Angus and

survived, the 15-year-old American hope, Ryan Harrison was beaten by Serbia's (another one!!) Filip Krajinovic, a qualifier.

On the girls side, the No.1 seed from American, Melanie Oudin was beaten in straight sets by Laura Robson, of Great Britain, which set home hearts a flutter; Arantxa Rus – named for the former world No.1 Arantxa Sanchez Vicario – was a Dutch girl of whom much hopes were being pinned, and she defeated Hong Kong's Zi-Jun Yang for the loss of three games. The oldies events were also ➤

starting to fire up and how good it was to see these wonderful practitioners back in action. One of their number, the immensely likeable Kevin Curren, of South Africa, was spotted on the players' lawn in deep conversation with Boris Becker, who had beaten him in the 1985 final that prompted a re-writing of the history books. What memories were invoked on seeing that pair together.

And the, of course there were hair-cuts to debate. Giles Smith had fun zeroing in on Jamie Murray, the mixed doubles champion, who was playing this year with Liezel Huber

of the United States rather than defending his crown with Jelena Jankovic who had declined this year's dance. He wrote: "Jamie is now officially the only player in the mixed draw whose hair is a topic of national conversation. He had been going – slightly against the fashionable grain, it must be said – for the John McEnroe look, straining his long locks (18 months in the growing, fact fans) through a red towelling headband. Now he's had an all-over No.3 and looks like a US Marine, fresh out of a Chinook. Now he's with Liezel Huber, born in South Africa but a naturalised

Venus Williams

American and a former Wimbledon champion in the women's doubles. That's Mrs Huber to you, by the way. And, one assumes, to Jamie. There's less hugging, is all I'm saying.

"And Jamie says their partnership is more businesslike. Actually, now he comes to mention it, all the pairings in the mixed doubles sound like businesses. Bryan and Srebotnik? They're an advertising agency, surely. Ullyet and Sugiyama? A Canadian capital investment bank. Lipsky and Dellacqua is a fashionable New York deli. Aspelin and Raymond make shirts. And

Tamarine Tanasugarn

Damm and Peng is what you say when you're in Lipsky and Dellacqua and you accidentally spill coffee down your best Aspelin and Raymond button-down."

Anyway, Murray and Huber were through to the fourth round, beating Austria's Julian Knowle and Yung-Jan Chan, of Taipei, 6-4 6-3, so the Murray family was prospering everywhere you looked. As was another.

Venus and Serena Williams were making emphatic strides towards a collision many had thought inevitable once so many of the grander stars departed the SW19 stage before the end of Act One. Venus was looking ever so well. Tamarine Tanasugarn, the stocky 31-year-old Thai had not dropped a set this year but had been beaten in their previous six meetings and finished, on all ocasions "as neatly parcelled up as a Thai takeaway," in the words of Ronald Atkin, the evergreen daily programme writer.

True to her form in the tournament thus far, Tanasugarn gave this her all, she often left Venus gaping at the crispness and variety of her shot-making off the ground but a smile was never far from her face, usually when she was left scrambling around in an attempt to reach some of the more powerful Williams shots.

Simon Barnes, the brilliant *Times* columnist said: "She (Venus) can turn it on – and off again. Afterwards she is an amiable flake with a silly voice; the roaring, whacking demon we saw on court has somehow vanished. She still sticks to the tactic that has served her well throughout her tennis life; that of overwhelming. She was serving at speeds well in excess of 120mph yesterday, saving her fiercest stuff for when she was break point down, a thing that champions tend to do. ➤

Zheng Jie

"I really expect it of myself." The shrieking was in good shape, the double-fister wasn't bad and the forehand is, as it always was, rather like a horse I used to ride: beautiful, immensely powerful and ever-so-slightly uncontrollable, dangerous to both opposition and owner."

Tanasugarn pushed her hard in the first set, persistent and accurate, and had five break points in a single service game. Each time, though, Williams blasted her way out of trouble, first-serving and second-serving with passion and purpose. "I think I love power," she said afterwards. She looked amazing under the clear blue Wimbledon skies: literally gleaming, the cheering sun picking vivid gold highlights from the generous acreage of skin revealed by her outfit. The abrasive, in-yer-face qualities she showed, when young, are muted now, her reluctance to follow tennis's code of manners more or less gone. She had even learned to apologise when she pulled out of a serve.

QUOTE of the Day

"Q. Are you aware of the last great British woman player?
A: I believe that was Virginia Wade or someone, quite a long time ago.

LAURA ROBSON, THE **14** YEAR OLD FROM GREAT BRITAIN, WHO WAS INTO THE THIRD ROUND OF THE GIRLS SINGLES.

Laura Robson

But the appetite had not gone. It is just intermittent and now that she is here, you can tell that she is ready to win it again, while those who pursue sport with the recommended single-mindedness can only wag their heads and wonder. "I don't have anything to prove," Venus said. "I'm very happy and blessed in my life."

So, indeed, was Zheng Jie. Take the mania surrounding Andy Murray, multiply it by ten and add the number you first thought of and you were getting close to the adulation that now surrounded the fifth-ranked Chinese player. And, upon her 6-2 5-7 6-1 victory over Nicole Vaidisova, of the Czech Republic, she disclosed that she would donate her portion of her Wimbledon winnings – and they would be at least £187,500 – to China's earthquake disaster fund in a gesture of astonishing generosity for a player whose total earnings this year had amounted £130,000.

Born in Cheng Du, the capital of the Szechuan province that had been devastated in the disasters earlier in the year, Zheng said she wanted desperately to help and, although the Chinese Tennis Federation took part of her winnings, she would give away her personal share. It was to be hoped she would make ➤

Nicole Vaidisova

Serena Williams

even more, though the redoubtable figure of Serena Williams would stand between her and the final. Serena defeated Agnieszka Radwanska of Poland, a former girls champion, 6-4, 6-0 in a match that was a match for one set only. The next day, an estimated 100 million people in China would follow both her progress and that of the irrepressible Miss Jie on television – the type of viewing figures the BBC would die for.

Now ensconced in the commentary box, Tim Henman was relishing his new role. He took time out this day to scout the practice courts, wondering how young Murray was preparing for his first grand slam tournament quarter-final. The four-times semi-finalist remarked: "Commentating on Andy's match [the five-set victory over Richard Gasquet, of France] on Monday, I was able to reflect on some of my matches and I feel as though I ought to be apologising for all the torture I put people through. I was so nervous watching it.

"When you are out there, you're in the moment, running around and somewhat in control of what's going on. But when there is nothing you can do, it is nerve-racking. There are facets to Andy's game he's obviously got to do well against Nadal. He needs to serve aggressively, you need cheap points from Nadal and they don't often come. From the baseline, you have to play aggressively to his forehand and open up the backhand. For me, Andy's attitude and demeanour has been first-class and the knock-on effect is the support he's had because the atmosphere on Monday was incredible.

"He's been able to raise his own standards because before, when he's been petulant on the court, it has been harder to support him. But he has been positive, even in the difficult moments, he's fought his way out and the crowds here have seen enough tennis to know what he's going through. The people are getting to know him as a person and player." ●

Agnieszka Radwanska

Day **NINE**
2.07.2008

NADAL
VS
MURRAY

FEDERER
VS
ANCIC

SAFIN
VS
LOPEZ

"He lost not because of his failings but because Nadal is a better tennis player." It was the summing up that struck the nail squarely on the head. Andy Murray, having given his considerable all after a two year absence from Wimbledon was beaten in his first grand slam quarter-final by a player at the height of his powers. Rafael Nadal defeated the British No.1 in straight sets, 6-3 6-2 6-4 and called it a special win. "Sorry for him," the Spaniard remarked as he departed Centre Court and you sincerely believed he was.

A stillness that only this particular court can muster had descended long before the conclusion of the third set, because the outcome had not been in doubt for some time. It is one thing convincing yourself that you can defeat someone of Nadal's class, something else entirely to make good on that conviction.

Rafael Nadal

John McEnroe

Andy Murray

Murray insisted that the physical effects of his victory over Richard Gasquet, of France, on Monday – and the consequent stirring of the nation – had no bearing, but maybe the mental fall-out from such excesses had taken a toll. The Scot did not chase around the court with the exuberance that had so demoralised Gasquet and was unable to raise his game to the levels that had generated such an extraordinary atmosphere on Monday night.

He had acknowledged, in its aftermath, that it would be his job to provide the spark that may ignite the home crowd against Nadal, but the world No.2 never gave him a chance. The sheer speed of Nadal's ground strokes had Murray constantly stretched and denied him the opportunity to adopt the attacking game that he had wanted to play.

Murray's returns are one of the strongest parts of his game, but he never got to grips with the pace and placement of the left-handed deliveries. The Spaniard won 88 per cent of his points on first serve and 80 per cent on second as Murray failed to force a single break point, winning only five points on Nadal's serve in the first two sets. His own serve was inconsistent and Nadal punished anything from him that lacking penetration. The world No.2 acknowledged that he had never played better at Wimbledon than he did in the first and second sets. "I played very aggressively all the time," he said. "Every time ➤

I tried to hit the ball close to the lines. I knew that if I played slowly it would be very difficult to beat Andy. To beat him you have to play at a higher rhythm than him."

There were a few things you could have carped at in Murray's performance: the desperate drop shot in the first set that helped to lead to the initial service break, a volleying error in the second that opened the door again. But to concentrate on such things was to miss the point. Nadal was playing a brand of power tennis that was virtually error-free, so it was right to salute the winner first. Only then was it proper to ask where the loser might go from here.

Murray has appreciated two significant lessons from these Championships – that he

QUOTE of the Day

"When you go through a match like that, not having to save a break-point and the other guy has to work extremely hard to win his service games, you know you're in a good and comfortable position. I mean, today I was in complete control. I was never really under pressure."

ROGER FEDERER BEAT MARIO ANCIC 6-1 7-5 6-4
AND, AS EVER, TOLD IT LIKE IT WAS.

Mario Ancic

could play his best on the biggest stage, that he could surf the wave of the Centre Court crowd's devotion and that that big stage was his natural environment. He had also discovered that to win a grand slam title he had a fair bit more to find in his game. The first thing he required was an honest assessment of the match and his performance. And Murray was heading the right way. Spurning the usual loser's clichés, he said: "He played so much better than me. He was playing too well for me. His forehand was ridiculous. I felt rushed on every point." He would surely return an even better player.

Before all that had unfurled, Roger Federer had come and gone and, this time, Mario Ancic was not going to make a monkey out of ➤

him. The last player to have defeated Federer on grass, in the first round of the 2002 Championships was back where he wanted to be, but then, so, too, was Federer. The great man's 6-1 7-5 6-4 victory was a 63rd consecutive on grass and 38th at Wimbledon stretching back to his Ancic moment. This was also a 17th grand slam semi-final in succession.

The first set was about as good as it could get, a 19-minute rout in which Federer conceded only one point off his own serve in four games. "I never saw him serving better," Ancic said, to which Federer responded: "I don't hardly practise it." At that point even his insouciance was sounding stretched. At 1-1 in the second set, the rain forced a two-hour delay. Was this a chance for Ancic to down some spinach and come out, biceps flexed, sustaining aggression. "I'm so proud of myself how I was doing in that second and third set," the Croat said. By which the 2004 semi-finalist meant that there was at least one game when he made Federer momentarily break into a sweat.

On his own serve, Ancic made one game stretch to 15 minutes, which was a victory in itself, but as the world No.1 rained down unanswerable serves and swatted backhands with piercing precision, the only reservation was that this tournament has still not seen how his game will withstand intense pressure.

That would, hopefully, arrive in the semi-finals where he would meet Marat Safin, in a repeat of their 2005 Australian Open meeting at the same juncture, a scintillating match that the Russian took in five sets en route to the title. Safin's defeat on No.1 court of Feliciano Lopez of Spain, 3-6 7-5 7-6 6-3, disclosed every facet of the complex man – nervous, exasperated, flamboyant, unplayable – and he became the first Russian ever to make the last four in SW19. ➤

Marat Safin

Lopez hails from Toledo, and had El Greco ever found such a man there he would certainly have painted him as St John. Those soulful eyes, and with hair cascading onto his shoulders, Lopez had recently made his acting debut in a Spanish soap opera. For Safin, however, melodrama was always reality. As early as the fifth game, his serve already broken, he was flinging his racket to the ground. Soon after, he took out his frustration on a ball, hitting it over the roof. At 2-5, the clouds wept at Safin's plight and offered him a chance to regroup. He had much to ponder during those two hours of solitude.

Eight years ago, at 20, he had the world at his feet. He had beaten Pete Sampras to win the US Open, and bought himself five cars. Sampras hailed the world's new No.1 as 'the future of tennis'. But to Safin, like Sergeant Troy, the past was yesterday, and the future tomorrow; never the day after. He kept changing his coach, kept getting injured, kept telling everyone that one day it would all come good. Playing on his wits, he remained capable of anything.

In 2005, he beat Lleyton Hewitt in the Australian Open final. He came here ranked 75 in the world, but peremptorily dispatched the third seed, Novak Djokovic, in the second round. At his best he would fancy his chances against anyone, even Federer. At worst? Well, he had won consecutive matches only three times this year before Wimbledon.

A very different Safin emerged from the break, levelling the match with some inspired tennis in the second set. Both men held serve obstinately through the third, but Safin's court coverage implied a growing belief. Sure enough, he won the tie-break, 7-1, and hope seemed to ebb from his opponent, whose service was broken early in the fourth. Lopez did save one match point, but wanly served a double fault on the second.

The way Safin has marauded into the last four is reminiscent of another volatile favourite, the Croat, Goran Ivanisevic, in 2001. According to another compatriot, Rudolf Nureyev, technique is what you fall back on when you run out of inspiration. Safin could doubtless have observed that axiom more

scrupulously over the years. At times like this, however, he is entitled to believe the inspiration will never run dry. Nadal, meanwhile, had to wait to discover who would be cast in the role of sacrificial lamb in his semi-final. Rainer Schuettler and Arnaud Clement were still contesting the privilege as the light faded and would resume the following day at one set apiece.

A final thought, though, on Murray who showed many things this Wimbledon. He had touch and finesse and stubbornness. He also had a tennis brain, a streak of honesty, a love of the limelight and some bouncy new muscles. He could serve deep and spitefully. He could play the drop shot beautifully (he could also play it foolishly). But the important thing he had shown was that he could find his best tennis at the toughest moments. That was something all champions possessed – for tennis is a sport that lends itself more than most to inspiration.   ●   **Rainer Schuettler and Arnaud Clement**

Day **TEN**
3.07.2008

ROBSON
VS
JOVANOVSKI

SCHUETTLER
VS
CLEMENT

S. WILLIAMS
VS
ZHENGH JIE

V. WILLIAMS
VS
DEMENTIEVA

Venus Williams serves to Elena Dementieva during their Women's semi-final on the Centre Court

Laura Robson

Thursday 3 July…

Malcolm Gracie, Charles Trippe and Sir Geoffrey Cass were all marching towards Court No.18 on women's semi-finals day. Why would these three eminent former presidents of the Lawn Tennis Association not be taking their snug seats on Centre Court rather than mixing it with the *hoi polloi*? Well, actually, they had time to kill before the 1pm start on the main show court and why not spend it luxuriating in a bit of British fun? After all, they had spent their years in the hot seat hoping for someone like Laura Robson to come along and now - blast it - someone else was going to get all the glory.

The stands for the quarter-finals of the girls singles were not usually this crowded but on strode Miss Robson, who was up against the No.9 seed, Bojana Jovanovski, of Serbia, who was going to be a tough opponent for she struck the ball with purpose and poise. But

Laura just had a bit too much in all aspects for her and won 7-5 6-4. Cue the back pages.

Crossing to No.1 court, there was still some men's quarter-final stuff to be completed. Rainer Schuettler and Arnaud Clement were returning to the fray, having been brought from the court as darkness fell the previous evening, tied at one set all. With Rafael Nadal already pawing at the practice courts with a view to Friday's semi-final, it was best that one or other of Schuettler and Clement would lay this match to rest as soon as possible.

And what happened? Only an epic, and one which ran for longer than Ben-Hur. Schuettler and Clement beat the living daylights out of each other. By the time they trudged off in need of a full day's rest, instead of half at best, they had traded multiple long rallies and umpteen breaks of serve in three more marathon sets. The final score read 6-3

5-7 7-6 6-7 8-6. The duration of the match, five hours and 12 minutes, had qualified it for joint second-longest in the history of the singles at the All England Club.

The record was held by Americans, Greg Holmes and the late, Todd Witsken, who competed for five hours and 28 minutes over three days in 1989's second round. Schuettler and Clement equalled in duration the famed Pancho Gonzales/Charlie Pasarell first round duel in 1969 that had also been interrupted on its first day by fading light and was played in the days before the advent of the tie-break.

Schuettler was contesting his 10th Wimbledon and had never previously reached the quarter-finals, and had been especially prone to injuries that contributed to his performances in the past two years, when he was beaten in the first round. Such was his dismay at his chances, he had intended to be spending this week at a Challenger event in Cordoba, Spain. "The match could have gone either way, I'm just happy to have made it through," said the 32-year-old of his win. "It's definitely one of the matches I will always remember." Schuettler agreed that Nadal would have an advantage but added, "He's pretty fit anyway, but I don't really care. I also work hard. I'm physically fit. I will get a massage and try to sleep early if possible to get enough hours. I'll be fine for the match." ➤

Arnaud Clement

Rainer Schuettler

There was something about Clement and feats of endurance. In 2004, the diminutive Frenchman featured in the longest match in grand slam history when he lost 16-14 in the final set to Fabrice Santoro, in the first round of the French Open, a match that lasted six hours and 33 minutes and caused the cancellation of many a restaurant reservation. This time, the 30-year-old Clement saved six successive set points after falling 6-0 down in the third-set tie-breaker before losing it with a double fault, but he came back to claim the fourth set and extend both everyone's nerves and the brilliance of some of the rallies.

It was to be Schuettler, the 2003 Australian Open finalist, who prevailed and joined Boris Becker and Michael Stich as Germany's men's Wimbledon semi-finalists in the Open Era. "I grew up watching Boris win Wimbledon so now I'm in the semis. I'm more than happy," he said.

And so to the supposed centre of attention, the ladies' semi-finals. And it was time, one thought, to give the Williams sisters their full dues. Serena Williams joined her sister, Venus, in the final after what was eventually a perfectly splendid semi-final. She beat Zheng Jie, of China, 6-2 7-6. Zheng was ranked No.133 to Williams's No.6, she was giving away four inches in height and a couple of stone in weight. ➤

Zheng Jie

Serena Williams

If we had not had rain delays - yes, it had started to rain at Wimbledon - we might have had a shock, because Zheng was moving Serena all over the court, hitting hard and low and flat and finding the corners. Williams does not care too much for the running about part of tennis — she is better at standing still and whacking the ball. She was beginning to look flustered and also a bit blown.

But the rain came and she got her breath back, and though she was taken to a tie-break in the second set, she served it out so ferociously that Zheng was blasted aside. The match ended on a double-fault, an unworthy way for Zheng to lose. She had been one of the great joys of this Wimbledon and her sharp-angled, two-fisted cross-courter was the most thrilling shot we had seen in the women's competition.

All the same, it was Williams who won, and it is Williams whom she would meet in the final, which was a cue for the inevitable groans and cynical suggestions that they will decide who wins over breakfast. Surely such thoughts were unworthy of sensible people. We should, instead, concentrate on the splendour that is the family Williams. The legend of the sisters' upbringing had not been exaggerated; Compton in Los Angeles really was not the place for a pleasant evening stroll.

That one world-class player should emerge from the cracked public tennis courts there was remarkable, that two should do so, and from the same family, was little short of a miracle.

True, they have been a bit abrasive at times, sometimes a bit awkward, sometimes a little rough about the edges. That was often the way with mould-breakers. Sometimes the ➤

sisters have seemed to treat the conventions of the game with contempt, trying to win the warm-up, overdoing the glares, not apologising for points won from a net-cord, getting too close at the change of ends. Little things, niggly things that added up. Their tennis had been pretty charmless, if pretty devastating. Each had a game that inspired admiration, rather than affection, for both played with little more than power, they liked to blast everything in their way.

The sisters lacked the sense of vulnerability that attended almost all tennis players, of either sex, even the best ones. That was because, uniquely, they were not alone. There were two of them, tight, loved and loving and that has been a source of extraordinary strength to them. And they go on and they go on, and here they were at Wimbledon and one of them was going to win it again.

Elena Dementieva had been standing in the way of Venus' attempt to reach her seventh Wimbledon final and when she trailed 4-0 in the first set, it appeared as if the Russian would not be erecting much of a roadblock. We had seen this from Dementieva before, she could either crush the ball to fine effect, or her brittle temperament would flare and Vera, her mother and constant travelling companion, would look as if fit to burst into tears.

Dementieva did pull her game together, enough to take the second set into a tie-break and suggest a fine battle but it did not quite materialise. At least, Dementieva could be certain of one thing, her ear-splitting scream which halted the traffic in Wimbledon Village when she netted one backhand in the breaker, would set the record as the most frightening of The Championships. She then went on in her press conference to suggest that the final might be decided over a 'family decision' which caused the sport's legislators to fly into a right old panic until it was stressed that she had lost something in translation. ●

Day ELEVEN
4.07.2008

FEDERER
vs
SAFIN

NADAL
vs
SCHUETTLER

SPEED OF SERVE
121MPH
www.wimbledon.org

Friday 4 July...

It is American Independence Day and, the following afternoon's final between Serena and Venus apart, where had all those Yanks disappeared to? Liz Clarke, the excellent columnist for the *Washington Post* reported to the All England Club's media committee that she felt this would be her final trip to SW19 – "because American newspapers are slowly dying and I can't see the trend being reversed. If I don't come one year and the trip is wiped from the budget, I don't think it will ever be put back," she said. Cue concerned faces all round.

Looking down the list of competitors, Serena and Venus were playing doubles, Bob and Mike Bryan likewise in the mixed (they were still in the gentlemen's doubles as well), Liezel Huber (South African-born but of US nationality) was in the ladies doubles and the mixed, and Bradley Klahn and Ryan Harrison were competing in the boys doubles. In the golden oldies events, Martina Navratilova (formerly of Czechoslovakia) and Ros Fairbank (formerly of South Africa), now US citizens, were competing.

There was a sense of shell-shock that American tennis was in a period of such travail. Even their better coaches – well, at least Paul Annacone and Brad Gilbert – had chosen to decamp to the British LTA, which offered the enormous incentive of substantial reward for part time work. One day soon perhaps the pendulum would swing back in their favour.

The men's singles – which had long since ceased to interest our American cousins – had reached semi-finals day which was always one that played on the nerves. On the players' lawn, Carlos Costa, Rafael Nadal's agent, had a cigarette but no means of lighting it, so he asked Dirk Hordoff, Rainer Schuettler's veteran coach, for a flame. Neither man's hand looked particularly steady. Semi-final days at grand slam tournaments tend to be like that.

The pair chattered amicably for a few seconds before Costa returned to his table where Nadal's father, Sebastian, sat, also holding onto a cigarette, which required kindling. His 22-year-old son's subsequent performance in reaching his third consecutive Wimbledon final was one of those that would have had plenty in his support group reaching for something to mollify the nerves.

Roger Federer was first up against Marat Safin, a reprise of their meeting in the 2005 Australian Open semi-final, which the Russian had won 9-7 in the fifth set, a monster of a match in which both men had been close to the peak of performance. It was ten months ➢

Marat Safin

earlier that Safin's management contacted Hernan Gumy, a Argentinian who reached a career high ranking of No.39 but never won a match on grass to ask if he might consider coaching their charge. Gumy had worked with Guillermo Canas and knew all about handling delicate situations and individuals, as he had to help Canas over the period of his career that was all but ruined by a 15-month suspension on a doping charge. Gumy met Safin in Los Angeles, took a look at him and decided a few home truths were an imperative if the partnership had any chance of working.

"What I heard from people before I knew Marat was that he was like a horse, it was very difficult to put him on the track but when I found him myself, I was really surprised," Gumy said. "At that meeting he said many people thought he was done, that he didn't care any more, that he had lost his mind for the game. I gave him my opinion, I saw a big guy but no muscles but a little fat. I said 'let's go from here, let's get back in shape as soon as possible and then let's see'.

"I noticed with his knee injury he had changed his strokes. His legs were too close and this is typical behaviour when you have trouble with your knee because you try to cover it with the other one, and it affects the way you play your forehand, the way you move your hips. I showed him a lot of videos from before and we saw a little bit of difference in every stroke. He kept saying 'I don't know what I'm doing, I've lost my game.' He was playing four metres behind the baseline and too much running. We were lucky to find all these things. We wanted to get back to the way he used to play."

Their period together has not been without its hazards. When Safin lost to relative unnotables like Bobby Reynolds (USA), Jurgen Melzer (Austria), Lee Hyung-Taik (Korea) and Robin Haase (The Netherlands), one imagined Gumy had to handle him as one would a piece of porcelain. "We don't talk to much when he loses," the coach said. "He isn't a guy who gets crazy, really. He does not want to lose, especially against players he would normally never lose to, but above all, I kept saying the same things, 'don't worry, keep working, sooner or later it will change'. He was getting in shape (Safin had put on six kilos and his biceps were a deal bigger than Andy Murray's) he was getting better, I was sure. He was getting a little desperate that it was not coming but he was still fighting and working hard."

But Federer did not waste much time and if the scoreline of 6-3 7-6 6-3 suggested Safin made a huge fist of it, there was a sense that he did not really get close. As Stephen Bierley reported in *The Guardian* "Great tennis matches demand high tension and, although

there were any number of superlative shots during Federer's 6-3 7-6 6-4 semi-final victory against Marat Safin, there was never the slightest feeling of an upset in the making. Indeed, for the majority of the match, the Russian, the former US and Australian Open champion, mooched around the Centre Court with the air of a man locked in internal torment who did not know from where the next point was coming."

The smashed racket – the sign that Safin had reached full smoulder, did not come until late on by which time Federer was into the last strides of a victory so clinical, so complete that the score of 6-3 7-6 6-4, compiled in one hour, 42 minutes, was not so much a record of events as a charitable understatement. "When you have a chance against Federer you have to go for it, but the trouble is that under the pressure he creates everyone makes mistakes – except Nadal," Safin said later. "That is the big difference between Federer and the rest of the players – and the rest of the players and Nadal. Who will win on Sunday? Oh, it's such a tough one – I don't know that there's ever been a tougher one."

On this day Federer broke Safin at the first opportunity so effortlessly you might have thought the threat from a younger and more menacing gun was the figment of disordered imagining. He made forehands that brought delayed applause, so startling and audacious were they in their conception and their execution. At one point in the third set, when the brief disturbance of the tie-break had been quelled, Federer casually flipped his racket through his legs for a very passable return. ➤

"I was feeling happy and very relaxed," said Federer. "Really my return to another final has been great. I was winning my service games pretty comfortably except for one stage in the second set. I was feeling very good and I was able to break him in the first game of the match and the last. I think, in between, I was just really consistent. I didn't really give him too many chances, so it was a perfect game for me."

After 23 minutes of the 'other' semi-final, between Nadal and Rainer Schuettler, it would have been wildly optimistic to have suggested that the German might win half a dozen games. "This has got the making of a tense classic," my neighbour in the press seats said, heavy on the irony. The excesses of Schuettler's two-day quarter-final against Arnaud Clement had clearly taken a toll – his legs would not move, he had to duck under a couple of Nadal serves. But consider playing someone ranked No.94 in the semi-finals when you have crushed the No.12, the local

favourite, in the quarter-finals. Something did not seem quite right.

Nadal hesitated and Schuettler is not that much of an old lag at 32 that he does not try to seize such opportunities. Unlike the breeze of a second set against Andy Murray, after which Nadal could not recall a better grass-court set, the second against Schuettler was among his least impressive. Indeed, the German served for it at 5-4, only for Nadal to play in the manner of the occasion. He broke back commandingly and snaffled the tie-break with a couple of the booming service winners he was going to have to replicate on final's day.

The third set was not plain sailing – Nadal rubbed his leg, cast anxious glances to his coaches and then skipped along the baseline to spin vicious forehand passes down the line. But nothing could deter him from the 6-1 7-6 6-4 victory and taking a step closer to what he has dreamed of since that afternoon 12 months ago when he was so close to beating Federer and was inconsolable at his inability to do so. ●

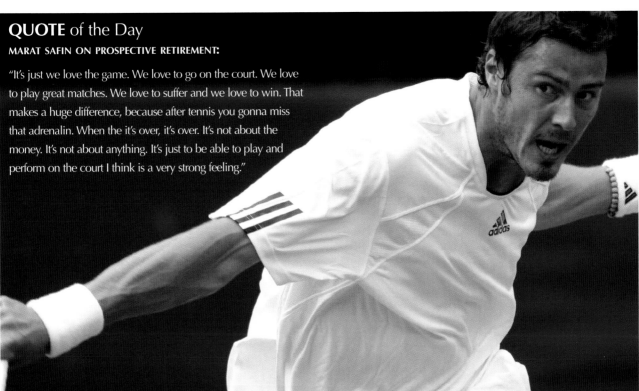

QUOTE of the Day

MARAT SAFIN ON PROSPECTIVE RETIREMENT:

"It's just we love the game. We love to go on the court. We love to play great matches. We love to suffer and we love to win. That makes a huge difference, because after tennis you gonna miss that adrenalin. When the it's over, it's over. It's not about the money. It's not about anything. It's just to be able to play and perform on the court I think is a very strong feeling."

Day **TWELVE**
5.07.2008

V. Williams
vs
S. Williams

Williams and Williams
vs
Raymond and Stosur

Bjorkman and Ulyett
vs
Nestor and Zimonjic

Robson
vs
Lertcheewakarn

Saturday 5 July…

Billie Jean King was one of the Chairman's special guests for The Championships and it was right and proper that she should have been accorded such Centre Court privileges as Venus and Serena Williams readied for the seventh sisterly act in a grand slam tournament final. Mrs King had won 20 Wimbledon titles in her extraordinary career and on what would be another historic day, Venus could be about to make it eight (five singles and three doubles) and Serena six (three singles and three doubles).

Catching up with Billie Jean was always an tricky endeavour for she rarely sat still for a moment, always things to do, people to see, wrongs to right. It was a case of being in the right place at the right time and then one spotted her, cross legged on the players' balcony, overlooking Court No.2 watching

(and doing a running commentary on) the Ladies Invitational Doubles that pitted Martina Navratilova and Helena Sukova against Ros Nideffer (nee Fairbank) and Ilana Kloss.

"Hey Neil, how's it goin?' she asked. "How's *this* going Billie Jean?" one replied.

Martina Navratilova sits in the Royal Box with Czech artist, Juraj Kralik, Billie Jean King and Ilana Kloss, before the Women's Singles final

"Some good shots, some bad, oh, c'mon Ilana, up the line, not crosscourt. Poor shot selection".

"I'm interested in your thoughts on Venus and Serena," I said.

"That's a hard one because they know each other so well but they are more mature these days," Mrs King replied and off she went. "Before, it was so much harder when they played each other… they have learned to play the ball and not think so much about who is on the other side… they are both injury free as well, which is a good thing… Venus loves it here, Serena has just this incredible will to win …Venus is more even tempered and introspective, Serena is so much more dramatic… I love them both… I remember hitting with them at a World Team Cup gig in Long Beach, California… their Mom and Dad brought them there…I remember Venus, especially, a gangly girl who was such an athlete… Oracene is quite a saint… she's so good when they're on court and after matches, she hugs them both as any Mom would…they are the best and they know it… that ball was in… what's wrong with the linesmen… clearly in." I left Mrs King to her doubles, notebook replenished.

The women's final had not had the greatest of build-ups, at least not one that might have been expected, considering the match-up ranked as one of the most prolific rivalries in grand slam finals, surpassed in the Open Era

only by Navratilova and Chris Evert's 14 major finals and matched by Steffi Graf and Arantxa Sanchez Vicario's seven.

There were the usual troublesome stories about breakfast table collusions but I had never believed such tosh. Perhaps when they were younger and Serena was in awe of her sister, she did not – could not – give of her best and these matches were disappointments but, as the years rolled by, and they had grown into big girls, such situations seemed far too preposterous for words. As it turned out, this was to be a final to savour, which Venus took 7-5 6-4 and, on balance, thoroughly deserved. It was an hour and 51 minutes brimful of passion, power and intensity. A cruel wind that gusted and swirled around Centre Court made things perilous for the server, but in the end Venus proved the more adept, beating her younger sister for the first time in a grand slam final since the 2001 US Open.

Twice previously, Venus had been forced to accept second best to Serena at Wimbledon's close and this could easily have been a third failure as she trailed by a break of serve in both sets. However, there has been a flint-eyed determination to the 28-year-old's play at this tournament, even when she was briefly troubled by Britain's Naomi Cavaday and Anne Keothavong in the initial two rounds, and such fortitude was apparent as she prevailed to studied applause.

Unlike her previous wins, there were no dances of delight, merely a broad grin up to Oracene, and a semi-curtsy of celebration. "Of course the celebration isn't as exciting," Venus said, "because my sister just lost. I'm ➤

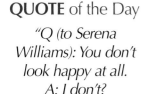

QUOTE of the Day

"Q (to Serena Williams): You don't look happy at all. A: I don't? I wonder why."

Serena Williams

Venus and Serena Williams celebrate after their victory in the Ladies' Doubles final

definitely thinking about how my sister's feeling." If the mood *sans* compassion Serena appeared to be demonstrating was a facade, she could be in line for numerous awards when she decides to pursue her acting career full-time. Serena did make a gift of one point after shrieking in the act of hitting a Venus serve, and Carlos Ramos, the Portuguese umpire, initially called a let. Until the touching embrace after a final backhand went wide on the second match point, there was little evidence of sisterly love.

There was no sign of the obligatory apology from Serena as the ball trickled over after flirting with the net cord. There were sighs of exasperation when Venus repeatedly pulled out of serves as the breeze buffeted her ball toss. Serena tried to intimidate by blazing one viciously hit backhand into her opponent's body, and when Venus tumbled when trying to turn wide in her backhand court, there was barely a look of concern. At one stage, Serena even questioned Ramos when she felt that her sibling was taking too long between points.

These two hit the ball harder than anyone in the women's game and the extended rallies saw the ball pummelled back and forth with groundstrokes full of venom. No quarter was asked for, none given, and if Elena Dementieva – suspicious of the sisters' competitive instincts in big matches against

each other after losing the semi-final to Venus two days earlier – had cared to watch, she would have had reason to reassess.

Nick Pitt, in the *Sunday Times* had a fascinating take on proceedings. "They did it," he wrote, "for there was plenty of competitive endeavour, loads of power, as well as some clenched fists. In fact, the wind was a bigger handicap to a quality encounter than sibling love. It swirled awkwardly around, so much in fact that one Serena lob went all round the parish before landing in court. Venus dispatched it with venom. Unlike so many of the leading women players left around today, she knows her way around a grass court. She can even volley.

But a good final could not cover up the depressing fact that women's tennis has gone back five years and more. Five years ago, the sisters contested the final. They were no better yesterday, but remain far ahead of the field when they put their minds to it, especially in the grass-court game. There was one difference between then and now. In 2003, they warmed up together under the supervision of their father, Richard. This time they had separate warm-ups. Richard had returned home to Florida, saying his job was done. "No matter what happens he's for sure going to be a winner," Serena said before the match, and of course he was. What he has ➤

Zimbabwe's Kevin Ullyett and Sweden's Jonas Bjorkman right, after losing the Men's Doubles final

won is not just Wimbledon; he has conquered the whole world of women's tennis. He did it long ago and he is still doing it. Take away his daughters, who are no longer full-time players, and you need to rummage around the cupboard to find anything worth watching."

They were worth watching in the doubles final, too, a double act of the highest order as they defeated Lisa Raymond, of the US, and Samantha Stosur, of Australia, 6-2 6-2, not the least bit exerted by the fact that this was their second match of the afternoon.

In between these two acts, there was to be no exultant end to his Wimbledon career for Jonas Bjorkman, the Swede who had announced his retirement during the first week. He and Kevin Ulyett, of Zimbabwe, gave of their best in the gentlemen's doubles but they were not equal to the vigorous challenge of Daniel Nestor and Nenad Zimonjic – the Canada/Serbian combination. Nestor, the left hander had lost in the 2002 final in the company of Mark Knowles and Zimonjic was twice a beaten finalist, in 2004 with Austrian, Julian Knowle, and two years later, with Fabrice Santoro, of France. Zimonjic had actually taken a terrible tumble in the semi-final and thought he had broken his wrist but he was in celebratory mood after a 7-6 6-7 6-3 6-3 victory.

Oh, and there was another match going on on Court No.1. The girls singles final, one that had attracted front and back page interest in

Britain. Never before had a 14-year-old British tennis player gained such notoriety and, this grand slam debutante, having beaten the No.1 seed, Melanie Oudin, of the United States, in the second round, was proving too adept for the third seeded Noppawan Lertcheewakarn of Thailand.

Australian-born, but very much a British citizen after moving to England as a six-year-old, Robson overcame a debilitating case of stage fright and a far more experienced opponent. The left-hander, who lives just a few hundred yards away from the Club gates, admitted: "Being Wimbledon junior champion sounds really, really good. It was so good today because all the crowd was behind me and it's just an overwhelming experience. But a couple of weeks ago, when Wimbledon started, if somebody had told me I would be champion I would have told them not to be stupid."

Warding off pressure from her Thai opponent, Robson, who was not to be 15 until January 2009 apeared relaxed and very composed, but the reality was different. "I thought I was going to be sick when I walked on court because there were so many people watching," she said. Showing undeniable competitive pedigree, she kept her nerve to win 6-3 3-6 6-1 and receive the trophy from 1969 Wimbledon champion, Ann Jones, who, at the age of 17, won the same title 52 years ago. The only disappointment was that Marat

Safin, on whom she said she had a teenage crush, had turned down her invitation join her at the Champions' Dinner.

He had already left London to play in the following week's tournament in Bastad, Sweden but left Laura a note which read: "To Laura, I'm sorry I couldn't come to the ball but good luck, Marat." She was not too heartbroken, admitting: "I think he's a bit too old for me, anyway." On a more serious note, Robson said she was looking forward to the award of a wild card into the main women's event next year. Asked how she fancied the prospect of facing Venus Williams in 2009, she replied with a cheeky smile: "I'll take her down." ●

Laura Robson

FINAL Day
6.07.2008

FEDERER
VS
NADAL

B. BRYAN AND STOSUR
VS
M. BRYAN AND
SREBOTNIK

DIMITROV
VS
KONTINEN

YANG AND HSIEH
VS
TOMIC AND REID

HERCOG AND MOORE
VS
HOLLAND AND PEERS

Sunday 6 July…

In 1886, two years after the first overseas competitors – James Dwight, Arthur Rives and Richard Sears of the United States – competed for the All England Championships, much was made of the fact that refreshments were to be served in the pavilion and, on Tuesday, July 13, Leamington's William Renshaw, at 25 years of age, won the title for a sixth time in succession, defeating Herbert Fortescue Lawford, who was ten years his elder, 6-0 5-7 6-3 6-4. This was their third men's final in a row.

New baths and showers had been installed at Worple Road by 1894. Luxuries proliferated. Wilfred Baddeley, aged 22, and Wicklow-born Joshua Pim, at 25, also competed for a third year running for the singles title. Pim won 10-8 6-2 8-6. Ninety-six years on, by which time the foreign legions had all but taken over the tournament, 23-year-old Boris Becker, of Germany, and Stefan Edberg, 24, were at each other's throats for the third final in a row. Edberg, the eternally self-effacing Swede, lost a two set lead before he prevailed 6-2 6-2 3-6 3-6 6-4.

Not since that day had the same two men competed for the men's singles for a third time but that is what we had on our plates on

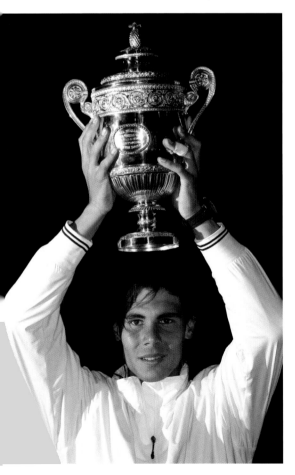

Sunday, July 6. This time it was Roger Federer, the 26-year-old five time champion against Spain's Rafael Nadal, who had recently turned 22 and had lost the two previous finals to the Swiss. Little did we know that what we were about to witness would transform all of our sporting perceptions.

Essentially, this was the final we'd expected to see from the moment the draw was made – actually a lot earlier than that, for it was hard to believe either of them would stumble unless something earth-shattering occurred. Now we had the final we wanted – Federer, the distinguished champion, bidding to surpass Bjorn Borg's five titles in a row and equal Renshaw's half-dozen. When Borg lost in his sixth final, it was to the No.2 seed, John McEnroe. Nadal, of course, was the No.2 seed. Federer would equal Borg's streak of 41 consecutive victories at Wimbledon if he won the final. Borg was in the front row, watching every move.

As one might have expected, the weather decided to take a change for the worse. Though the wind was coming in from the south, it contained a bitter chill for July. It was

QUOTE of the Day

"I wish, obviously, it was me with the trophy, but that's the way it is. This is probably my hardest loss, by far. I mean, it's not much harder than this right now, so…"
ROGER FEDERER

performance at the pre-final press conference, where he pulled his cap down low across his eyes and he seemed reluctant to talk, was in some way a sign of anxiety. Perhaps they were deluding themselves.

Nadal's single break in the first set was enough to secure that set, although Federer had a couple of chances to bring it back to 5-5 and this was where we began to appreciate the depth of his anxiety. A forehand volley was prodded long on the first opportunity and the second, a 91mph dolly of a second serve, was spun feebly into the net. First blood to Nadal. The Swiss response was as one might have expected, for he snaffled Nadal's opening service game and things were going swimmingly when he led 4-1, having only given up two points on serve in the set. Then, Nadal suddenly reached one of Federer's finest off-forehands, sending back a forehand riposte so vicious that Federer bent double, managed to make contact but to no avail. That was enough of an invitation for Nadal. ➤

Bjorn Borg

one of those days when gray cirrus skimmed across the sight-line in ill-tempered batches, a few spots of rain here, a drier patch there. There would probably be a delayed start, though the meteorological bods seemed certain there wuld be enough fine weather and visibility to complete the final on schedule. At 2.20, they emerged.

The first point of the match was a fluent rip-snorter and many of the 412 that followed it retained a similar pattern. This was the final we had hoped it would be, one that you could not take your eyes off for a minute, in case something else extraordinary happened. Federer should not have lost either of the first two sets and yet was two sets down – something that had only happened to him twice before in a grand slam tournament. Nadal should never have lost the fourth-set tie-break and yet they entered a fifth and final act. Was it ever going to be any other way?

Federer had not lost a set on grass since the final of the French Open, indeed break points against him were hard to find, and so he entered the for the last time in 2008 in a state of grace. The Spaniards wondered whether his

The Spaniard might have been 40-0 up in the next game but, after an extraordinary rally of twists, turns and pirouettes, he tried a drop shot and failed. Federer had a break point, but Nadal smacked a forehand winner. At deuce, with the court begging and the ball gently arcing towards Federer's racket, one of his fan club in their RF embossed hats, screamed: "Come on!". It was a cry that disturbed Federer to the extent that he missed wildly.

"Shut up!" he screamed back, but the damage had been done. Nadal held once more and, on the second break point in the next Federer service game, hit a remarkable forehand winner from a ball that stopped and spun on the baseline like a Shane Warne googly. And so Nadal was serving for the set. At 30-all, he received a time violation, the only such call of the match. What was Pascal Maria, the otherwise immaculate French umpire, thinking? Why then? Had he taken appreciably longer over his ball bouncing, did he pick at his pants once more than before? No. A poor call at, potentially, a critical point.

A beautiful backhand sliced winner brought up one set point, but Nadal then netted a forehand. Federer had a break point only for another stupefying rally to end with a tame backhand. A second set point to Nadal, another netted Federer backhand. Two sets to love for the challenger. If trepidation was filling the Swiss's heart, he did not let it show.

There were no physical scars, but his shoulders momentarily drooped. He had never been in this position in a Wimbledon final before and Nadal, in such a situation, normally mangled his prey.

But Federer said he could never give in, no matter where or when. A player who had won 12 grand slam finals did not stop believing, never stopped telling himself that he could win, whatever the circumstances. And this, after all, was his patch. His fiefdom. It was now beginning to become so dark that it was just as well Wimbledon had never considered dropping its predominantly white clothing policy. The players peered into the gloom, trying to pick their opponent's better shots.

Nadal saved four break points in a nine-minute sixth game and when Federer was 40-0 down in the next, surely the match was the Spaniard's for the taking. Nadal netted a backhand crosscourt, then Federer managed a service winner. Then a fault. A second serve sat up and begged to be put away. Nadal scuffed it into the net. Instead of 4-3 to Nadal, it was 4-3 to Federer. Nadal held, so did Federer, it started to rain. Off they went.

Who woud cope with the delay the better? It was the talk of the next 80 minutes. Nadal knew he had to serve to stay in the set, led 40-0, was dragged back to deuce, it went to ➤

Rafael Nadal is congratulated by Spain's Crown Prince Felipe and Princess Letizia

deuce again but he survived. And so to a tie-break that was dominated by the Federer serve, four aces in all. He was back. The fourth set did not include a single service break and so into another tie-break we went. Federer won the first point, against the serve with a flashing forehand down the line after Nadal had spun in the air in an attempt to land a high backhand volley. But the response was typical, two mini breaks, followed by an ace, a service winner and Nadal was 5-2 ahead, two points from glory.

His first serve was netted, the second touched the tape and landed on the wrong side. A double fault. Then he netted a routine backhand. Federer was alive again and actually sneaked a set point of his own, only to miss a forehand into the sidelines. Two of the following three points will live in Wimbledon folklore. A scintillating forehand pass by Nadal set up a first championship point; he could not have placed his subsequent serve any better, nor the follow up cross-court forehand that darted away from him but Federer, living on the edge, planted the most exquisite of backhand flicks into the corner. The force had return to his forearm and Nadal's backhand service return, that landed long, meant we stood at two sets all.

At 2-2, deuce, it rained once more, though the portents were for a swift resumption and, 15 minutes later, they were locked again. At 3-4, Nadal survived a break point with a telling smash – no sweaty palms there. At 5-5,

it was Federer's turn to live dangerously, two break points, the first saved with (what else?) an ace, the second when Nadal could only lash at a forehand and send it long. At 6-6, Federer was love-30 and pulled it out. At 7-7, he could not fashion a repeat, though it took Nadal four chances (two of them saved by aces) before he induced an error on the normally infallible forehand.

All Nadal had to do was serve for the title. Love-15 became 15-all when, heavens preserve us, the Spaniard served and volleyed. 30-15 became 30-all when Nadal stuck out a racket to a Federer shot that would have landed at the centre-service linesman's feet, first bounce. 40-30. Match point No.3. Once again Nadal's leftie serve arced to the backhand but Federer got enough on the response, cross court, that it spun from the rim of the Nadal racket into the crowd. A service winner brought up match point No.4. The roar was deafening. Nadal steadied, served, a forehand response, a three-quarter backhand down the middle and Federer, on his favoured side, sent the ball into the net. Nadal was flat on his back. Let joy be overflowing.

Two of Britain's finest sports writers had their take. Paul Hayward in the *Daily Mail* wrote: "After an insanely dramatic struggle that threatened to go on until the 2012 Olympics need these courts, people stumbled away with memories that will burn in them forever. This was the gift that these two great players left us with."

In the *Independent*, James Lawton offered these words. "So does this mean we are bound to revisit Wimbledon on Sunday night and concede we might just have got a little carried away when Nadal and Federer fought out what John McEnroe and Rod Laver believe to be the best Wimbledon final anyone has ever seen? You may think that it needs to be done, if only as a mark of respect to all those who had gone before, men like Laver and Borg and McEnroe and Sampras and, perhaps not least, Goran Ivanisevic, who came as a wild card after three final defeats and distilled all his passion for the game into an unforgettable victory over the formidable Australian, Pat Rafter. But then I don't.

"Indeed, the stronger inclination is to return to SW19 and hoist a flag or plant a tree and reaffirm that here, on Sunday 6 July 2008, we not only saw the greatest tennis match ever played, we were also given, cleanly, beautifully, the very essence of all that is best in sport and in a way I had never quite seen before and do not confidently expect ever to see again."

Believe it or not, there was tennis being played elsewhere. On No.1 Court, one of the famed Bryan twins, Bob, the left hander, became a mixed doubles champion for the first time, in partnership with Samantha Stosur, of Australia. It had to be that Mike, the right hander, was on the opposite side, with Katerina Srebotnik, of Slovenia. Bob and Sam won 7-5 6-4.

Laura Robson's victory in the girls' singles (see preceding pages) was matched in the boys by Grigor Dimitrov, of Bulgaria, the No.9 seed, who defeated the unseeded Finn, Henri Kontinen, 7-5 6-3. The boys doubles brought a stunning a success for Chinese Taipei in the shape of Tsung-Hua Yang and Cheng-Peng Hsieh, who defeated third seeds, Bernard Tomic and Matt Reid of Australia, 6-4, 2-6, 12-10. The girls doubles was a triumph for Polona Hercog, of Slovenia and Jessica Moore, of Australia, 6-3 1-6 6-2 over two other Australians, Isabella Holland and Sally Peers.

How wonderful, as ever, to see the old faces in such fine fettle. A pity that Jacco Eltingh and Paul Haarhuis, of Holland, the holders, could not compete in the final of the Over-35 Gentleman's Invitational Doubles and so the trophy went to Don Johnson and Jared Palmer from the United States. Martina Navratilova could not quite add to her Wimbledon haul, for she and Helena Sukova, of the Czech Republic, lost in the Ladies Invitational Doubles to Jana Novotna and Kathy Rinaldi-Stunkel 5-7 6-3 10-5.

The Gentleman's Senior Invitational Doubles (my heaven doesn't that sound ancient!) went to Ken Flach and Robert Seguso of the USA – twice champions in the men's doubles – who just held off the spirited Briton, Jeremy Bates and Anders Jarryd, of

Sweden 7-6 6-7 10-7. A word, too, for Mansour Bahrami, the moustachioed Iranian, who once more showed what a delightfully gifted entertainer he is.

Wheelchair tennis goes from strength to strength, as does Holland's supremacy at it on these lawns. Robin Ammerlaan and Ronald Vink retained their doubles title, defeating Stephane Houdet and Nicolas Peifer, of France, 6-7 6-1 6-3.

Bob Bryan, of the US, and Australia's Samantha Stosur after winning the Mixed Doubles

Slovenia's Polona Hercog (right) and Australia's Jessica Moore celebrate their Girls Doubles Final victory

Grigor Dimitrov, of Bulgaria, with the Boys Singles trophy

Rafael Nadal
The Gentlemen's Singles

Venus Williams
The Ladies' Singles

Nenad Zimonjic & Daniel Nestor
The Gentlemen's Doubles

Venus Williams & Serena Williams
The Ladies' Doubles

Bob Bryan & Samantha Stosur
The Mixed Doubles

Ronald Vink & Robin Ammerlaan
The Wheelchair Gentlemen's Invitation Doubles

Polona Hercog & Jessica Moore
The Girls' Doubles

Cheng-Peng Hsieh & Tsung-Hua Yang
The Boys' Doubles

Robert Seguso & Ken Flach
The Gentlemen's Senior Invitation Doubles

Kathy Rinaldi & Jana Novotna
The Ladies' Invitation Doubles

Grigor Dimitrov
The Boys' Singles

Laura Robson
The Girls' Singles

Donald Johnson & Jared Palmer
The Gentlemen's Invitation Doubles Winners
Walkover

145

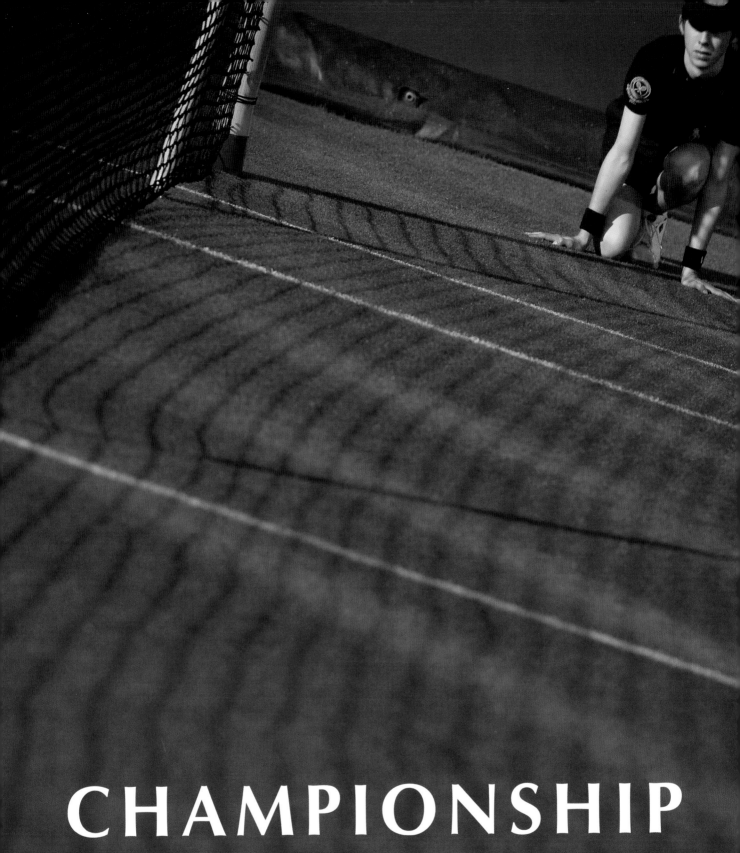

CHAMPIONSHIP
RECORDS
2008

EVENT I – THE GENTLEMEN'S SINGLES CHAMPIONSHIP 2008

HOLDER: R. FEDERER

The Winner became the holder, for the year only, of the CHALLENGE CUP presented by The All England Lawn Tennis and Croquet Club in 1887. The Winner received a silver replica of the Challenge Cup. A Silver Salver was presented to the Runner-up and a Bronze Medal to each defeated Semi-finalist. The matches were the best of five sets.

First Round

	1.	**Federer, Roger [1]** *(1)* (SUI)
	2.	Hrbaty, Dominik (70) (SVK)
	3.	Soderling, Robin (41) (SWE)
(Q)	4.	Kim, Kevin (181) (USA)
	5.	Gicquel, Marc (53) (FRA)
	6.	Nishikori, Kei (103) (JPN)
	7.	Guccione, Chris (77) (AUS)
(LL)	8.	Bozoljac, Ilia (197) (SRB)
	9.	**Hewitt, Lleyton [20]** *(27)* (AUS)
	10.	Haase, Robin (64) (NED)
	11.	Montanes, Albert (69) (ESP)
	12.	Berlocq, Carlos (90) (ARG)
(WC)	13.	Bogdanovic, Alex (242) (GBR)
	14.	Bolelli, Simone (46) (ITA)
	15.	Ginepri, Robby (59) (USA)
	16.	**Gonzalez, Fernando [15]** *(14)* (CHI)
	17.	**Berdych, Tomas [11]** *(20)* (CZE)
	18.	Korolev, Evgeny (78) (RUS)
	19.	Hanescu, Victor (81) (ROU)
	20.	Falla, Alejandro (106) (COL)
	21.	Sela, Dudi (66) (ISR)
	22.	Rochus, Olivier (67) (BEL)
	23.	Kohlschreiber, Philipp (36) (GER)
	24.	**Verdasco, Fernando [22]** *(18)* (ESP)
	25.	**Llodra, Michael [32]** *(34)* (FRA)
	26.	Ancic, Mario (43) (CRO)
	27.	Lee, Hyung-Taik (56) (KOR)
(Q)	28.	Petzschner, Philipp (118) (GER)
	29.	Andreev, Igor (37) (RUS)
	30.	Vanek, Jiri (82) (CZE)
(Q)	31.	Stakhovsky, Sergiy (135) (UKR)
	32.	**Ferrer, David [5]** *(5)* (ESP)
	33.	**Djokovic, Novak [3]** *(3)* (SRB)
	34.	Berrer, Michael (91) (GER)
	35.	Safin, Marat (75) (RUS)
	36.	Fognini, Fabio (86) (ITA)
	37.	Serra, Florent (74) (FRA)
	38.	Lu, Yen-Hsun (71) (TPE)
(LL)	39.	Kamke, Tobias (195) (GER)
	40.	**Seppi, Andreas [29]** *(30)* (ITA)
	41.	**Ferrero, Juan Carlos [21]** *(23)* (ESP)
	42.	Querrey, Sam (42) (USA)
(Q)	43.	Peya, Alexander (191) (AUT)
	44.	Zverev, Mischa (92) (GER)
	45.	Del Potro, Juan Martin (62) (ARG)
(Q)	46.	Snobel, Pavel (220) (CZE)
	47.	Daniel, Marcos (76) (BRA)
	48.	**Wawrinka, Stanislas [13]** *(9)* (SUI)
	49.	**Baghdatis, Marcos [10]** *(25)* (CYP)
	50.	Darcis, Steve (51) (BEL)
	51.	Johansson, Thomas (63) (SWE)
	52.	Spadea, Vincent (99) (USA)
	53.	Bellucci, Thomaz (68) (BRA)
	54.	Kunitsyn, Igor (79) (RUS)
(Q)	55.	Stadler, Simon (172) (GER)
	56.	**Karlovic, Ivo [18]** *(22)* (CRO)
	57.	**Lopez, Feliciano [31]** *(35)* (ESP)
	58.	Dabul, Brian (113) (ARG)
	59.	Karanusic, Roko (111) (CRO)
	60.	Horna, Luis (93) (PER)
	61.	Volandri, Filippo (120) (ITA)
	62.	Reynolds, Bobby (102) (USA)
	63.	Dancevic, Frank (95) (CAN)
	64.	**Nalbandian, David [7]** *(7)* (ARG)
	65.	**Roddick, Andy [6]** *(6)* (USA)
	66.	Schwank, Eduardo (60) (ARG)
	67.	Tipsarevic, Janko (40) (SRB)
	68.	Ascione, Thierry (119) (FRA)
	69.	Pashanski, Boris (114) (SRB)
(Q)	70.	Eaton, Chris (661) (GBR)
	71.	Mahut, Nicolas (58) (FRA)
	72.	**Tursunov, Dmitry [25]** *(33)* (RUS)
	73.	**Almagro, Nicolas [19]** *(12)* (ESP)
	74.	Granollers, Marcel (52) (ESP)
	75.	Garcia-Lopez, Guillermo (104) (ESP)
(Q)	76.	Van Der Merwe, Izak (285) (RSA)
	77.	Ventura, Santiago (88) (ESP)
	78.	Schuettler, Rainer (94) (GER)
(Q)	79.	Rochus, Christophe (112) (BEL)
	80.	**Blake, James [9]** *(8)* (USA)
	81.	**Mathieu, Paul-Henri [14]** *(16)* (FRA)
	82.	Hernandez, Oscar (107) (ESP)
(WC)	83.	Chardy, Jeremy (108) (FRA)
(Q)	84.	Gil, Frederico (110) (POR)
(Q)	85.	Roger-Vasselin, Edouard (147) (FRA)
	86.	Cilic, Marin (55) (CRO)
	87.	Odesnik, Wayne (87) (USA)
	88.	**Nieminen, Jarkko [24]** *(28)* (FIN)
	89.	**Ljubicic, Ivan [26]** *(31)* (CRO)
	90.	Melzer, Jurgen (72) (AUT)
(Q)	91.	Levine, Jesse (137) (USA)
	92.	Young, Donald (85) (USA)
	93.	Bjorkman, Jonas (128) (SWE)
	94.	Clement, Arnaud (145) (FRA)
	95.	Becker, Benjamin (116) (GER)
	96.	**Davydenko, Nikolay [4]** *(4)* (RUS)
	97.	**Gasquet, Richard [8]** *(10)* (FRA)
	98.	Fish, Mardy (39) (USA)
	99.	Grosjean, Sebastien (61) (FRA)
	100.	Starace, Potito (57) (ITA)
	101.	Anderson, Kevin (98) (RSA)
	102.	Calleri, Agustin (49) (ARG)
(Q)	103.	Olejniczak, Dawid (202) (POL)
	104.	**Simon, Gilles [28]** *(29)* (FRA)
	105.	**Robredo, Tommy [23]** *(19)* (ESP)
	106.	Vliegen, Kristof (109) (BEL)
	107.	Canas, Guillermo (44) (ARG)
	108.	Haas, Tommy (38) (GER)
(WC)	109.	Malisse, Xavier (226) (BEL)
	110.	Gremelmayr, Denis (80) (GER)
	111.	Santoro, Fabrice (54) (FRA)
	112.	**Murray, Andy [12]** *(11)* (GBR)
	113.	**Stepanek, Radek [16]** *(15)* (CZE)
(Q)	114.	Hernych, Jan (134) (CZE)
	115.	Troicki, Viktor (89) (SRB)
	116.	Lapentti, Nicolas (65) (ECU)
(WC)	117.	Baker, Jamie (268) (GBR)
(Q)	118.	Galvani, Stefano (201) (ITA)
	119.	Roitman, Sergio (97) (ARG)
	120.	**Youzhny, Mikhail [17]** *(17)* (RUS)
	121.	**Kiefer, Nicolas [27]** *(32)* (GER)
	122.	Benneteau, Julien (47) (FRA)
	123.	Vassallo Arguello, Martin (84) (ARG)
	124.	Minar, Ivo (70) (CZE)
	125.	Isner, John (83) (USA)
	126.	Gulbis, Ernests (48) (LAT)
(Q)	127.	Beck, Andreas (122) (GER)
	128.	**Nadal, Rafael [2]** *(2)* (ESP)

Second Round

R.Federer [1] 6/3 6/2 6/2
R.Soderling 7/5 0/6 6/3 6/4
M.Gicquel 4/6 7/5 0/0 Ret'd
I.Bozoljac 3/6 6/4 6/4 6/3
L.Hewitt [20] 6/7(4) 6/3 6/3 6/7(1) 6/2
A.Montanes 6/3 7/6(2) 6/4
S.Bolelli 7/6(4) 4/6 6/3 7/6(4)
F.Gonzalez [15] 7/6(3) 7/5 7/5
T.Berdych [11] 4/6 6/1 6/4 3/6 7/5
V.Hanescu 6/3 6/7(2) 6/0 6/4
O.Rochus 6/4 7/5 6/4
F.Verdasco [22] 6/4 6/3 6/2
M.Ancic 6/4 7/6(7) 2/0 Ret'd
P.Petzschner 6/7(4) 6/1 6/4 0/0 Ret'd
I.Andreev 6/7(6) 7/6(2) 6/2 6/2
D.Ferrer [5] 7/6(6) 6/3 1/3 Ret'd
N.Djokovic [3] 7/5 2/6 6/3 6/0
M.Safin 6/1 6/2 7/6(3)
F.Serra 6/4 6/4 6/7(3) 6/3
A.Seppi [29] 5/7 6/3 6/2 6/4
J.C.Ferrero [21] 2/6 6/4 6/4 6/4
M.Zverev 6/3 6/4 6/4
J.Del Potro 6/4 6/2 6/3
S.Wawrinka [13] 6/3 6/2 7/5
M.Baghdatis [10] 6/3 6/2 6/7(5) 6/3
T.Johansson 6/7(8) 6/7(5) 6/3 6/4 6/3
T.Bellucci 7/6(5) 7/6(5) 3/6 6/2
S.Stadler 4/6 7/6(4) 6/3 7/5
F.Lopez [31] 7/6(1) 3/6 6/3 6/4
R.Karanusic 7/6(4) 6/3 6/1
B.Reynolds 6/2 6/2 0/0 Ret'd
F.Dancevic 6/4 6/2 6/4
A.Roddick [6] 7/5 6/4 7/6(0)
J.Tipsarevic 7/6(4) 6/4 6/2
C.Eaton 6/3 7/6(6) 6/4
D.Tursunov [25] 6/4 6/7(8) 7/6(7) 3/6 7/5
N.Almagro [19] 4/6 6/3 7/5 6/2
G.Garcia-Lopez 7/5 6/2 6/2
R.Schuettler 6/3 6/2 6/4
J.Blake [9] 3/6 6/3 6/1 6/4
P-H.Mathieu [14] 3/6 6/2 6/0 6/2
J.Chardy 7/5 6/7(1) 4/6 6/4 6/3
M.Cilic 6/4 6/3 7/6(4)
J.Nieminen [24] 6/3 0/0 Ret'd
J.Melzer 6/4 7/6(7) 4/6 2/6 6/3
J.Levine 4/6 6/2 6/3 6/4
A.Clement 4/6 7/6(2) 6/4 7/6(4)
B.Becker 6/4 6/4 6/4
R.Gasquet [8] 6/3 6/4 6/2
S.Grosjean 6/2 7/5 6/1
A.Calleri 4/6 7/5 7/5 6/1
G.Simon [28] 6/3 6/4 6/2
T.Robredo [23] 6/1 6/3 6/7(4) 6/4
T.Haas 3/6 6/4 6/4 6/4
X.Malisse 6/3 6/4 6/2
A.Murray [12] 6/3 6/4 7/6(5)
R.Stepanek [16] 6/3 7/5 6/0
V.Troicki 6/3 4/0 Ret'd
S.Galvani 6/4 6/2 6/3
M.Youzhny [17] 6/1 6/4 6/0
N.Kiefer [27] 6/1 7/5 6/3
M.Vassallo Arguello 6/4 2/6 2/6 6/2 6/2
E.Gulbis 7/5 7/5 6/7(3) 7/6(6)
R.Nadal [2] 6/4 6/4 7/6(0)

Third Round

R.Federer [1] 6/3 6/4 7/6(3)
M.Gicquel 4/6 5/7 7/6(1) 7/6(0) 6/3
L.Hewitt [20] 7/6(4) 6/0 6/2
S.Bolelli 7/6(8) 7/6(7) 3/6 7/6(4)
T.Berdych [11] 6/7(5) 7/6(6) 6/1 6/2
F.Verdasco [22] 7/6(4) 6/7(5) 6/1 6/1
M.Ancic 6/1 6/4 6/7(1) 4/6 6/3
D.Ferrer [5] 3/6 6/3 6/4 6/2
M.Safin 6/4 7/6(3) 6/2
A.Seppi [29] 6/3 6/7(4) 6/2 6/7(5) 6/4
M.Zverev 6/4 6/4 2/1 Ret'd
S.Wawrinka [13] 7/6(5) 6/3 7/5
M.Baghdatis [10] 6/4 6/4 6/4
S.Stadler 3/6 6/3 6/1 6/7(5) 8/6
F.Lopez [31] 6/3 6/3 6/4
B.Reynolds 4/6 7/6(10) 6/4 6/4
J.Tipsarevic 6/7(5) 7/5 6/4 7/6(4)
D.Tursunov [25] 7/6(2) 6/2 6/4
G.Garcia-Lopez 6/3 3/6 5/7 6/1 6/2
R.Schuettler 6/3 6/7(8) 4/6 6/4 6/4
P-H.Mathieu [14] 6/3 7/5 7/6(1)
M.Cilic 6/4 3/6 6/3 6/7(6) 7/5
J.Melzer 4/6 6/2 3/6 6/4 6/1
A.Clement 7/6(7) 7/6(3) 6/3
R.Gasquet [8] 6/2 6/2 0/0 Ret'd
G.Simon [28] 5/7 6/2 6/3 6/4
T.Haas 6/4 6/4 6/3
A.Murray [12] 6/4 6/2 6/2
R.Stepanek [16] 6/7(1) 6/7(3) 6/3 6/1 6/2
M.Youzhny [17] 4/6 6/4 6/3 3/6 6/3
N.Kiefer [27] 6/0 6/3 6/1
R.Nadal [2] 5/7 6/2 7/6(2) 6/3

Fourth Round

R.Federer [1] 6/3 6/3 6/1
L.Hewitt [20] 6/1 6/3 7/6(2)
F.Verdasco [22] 6/4 6/4 6/0
M.Ancic 6/4 6/4 6/7(5) 7/6(3)
M.Safin 7/6(5) 3/6 7/6(3) 6/4
S.Wawrinka [13] 7/5 6/1 0/0 Ret'd
M.Baghdatis [10] 7/6(2) 6/4 6/2
F.Lopez [31] 6/4 7/5 4/6 6/4
J.Tipsarevic 7/6(1) 7/6(3) 6/3
R.Schuettler 6/2 6/3 6/4
M.Cilic 6/7(5) 6/3 6/4 7/6(7)
A.Clement 4/6 6/3 6/4 6/4
R.Gasquet [8] 6/3 6/3 6/7(3) 6/3
A.Murray [12] 6/4 6/7(4) 6/3 6/2
M.Youzhny [17] 7/5 6/7(5) 6/4 6/7(4) 6/3
R.Nadal [2] 7/6(3) 6/2 6/3

Quarter-Finals

R.Federer [1] 7/6(7) 6/2 6/4
M.Ancic 3/6 4/6 6/3 6/4 13/11
M.Safin 6/4 6/3 5/7 6/1
F.Lopez [31] 5/7 6/2 3/6 7/6(4) 8/6
R.Schuettler 6/4 3/6 6/4 7/6(4)
A.Clement 6/3 7/5 6/2
A.Murray [12] 5/7 3/6 7/6(3) 6/2 6/4
R.Nadal [2] 6/3 6/3 6/1

Semi-Finals

R.Federer [1] 6/1 7/5 6/4
M.Safin 3/6 7/5 7/6(1) 6/3
R.Schuettler 6/3 5/7 7/6(6) 6/7(7) 8/6
R.Nadal [2] 6/3 6/2 6/4

Final

R.Federer [1] 6/3 7/6(3) 6/4
R.Nadal [2] 6/1 7/6(3) 6/4

Winner

R.Nadal 6/4 6/4 6/7(5) 6/7(8) 9/7

Heavy type denotes seeded players. The figure in brackets against names denotes the order in which they were seeded.
The figures in italics denotes ATP Ranking – 26/06/2007 (WC)=Wild card. (Q)=Qualifier. (LL)=Lucky loser.

EVENT II – THE GENTLEMEN'S DOUBLES CHAMPIONSHIP 2008
HOLDERS: A. CLEMENT & M. LLODRA

The Winners became the holders, for the year only, of the CHALLENGE CUPS presented by the OXFORD UNIVERSITY LAWN TENNIS CLUB in 1884 and the late SIR HERBERT WILBERFORCE in 1937. The Winners received a silver replica of the Challenge Cup. A Silver Salver was presented to each of the Runners-up, and a Bronze Medal to each defeated Semi-finalist. The matches were the best of five sets.

First Round

1. **B.Bryan** (USA) & **M.Bryan** (USA) [1]
(WC) 2. C.Eaton (GBR) & A.Slabinsky (GBR)

3. J.Levinsky (CZE) & D.Skoch (CZE)
4. I.Kunitsyn (RUS) & D.Tursunov (RUS)

5. C.Berlocq (ARG) & E.Schwank (ARG)
6. G.Canas (ARG) & M.Garcia (ARG)

(WC) 7. R.Bloomfield (GBR) & K.Skupski (GBR)
8. **F.Cermak** (CZE) & **J.Kerr** (AUS) [13]

9. **M.Fyrstenberg** (POL) & **M.Matkowski** (POL) [10]
10. R.Bopanna (IND) & A-U-H.Qureshi (PAK)

11. S.Ratiwatana (THA) & S.Ratiwatana (THA)
12. M.Granollers (ESP) & S.Ventura (ESP)

13. T.Bellucci (BRA) & M.Daniel (BRA)
(Q) 14. P.Pala (CZE) & I.Zelenay (SVK)

(Q) 15. F.Gil (POR) & D.Norman (BEL)
(LL) 16. H.Armando (USA) & J.Levine (USA)

17. **M.Bhupathi** (IND) & **M.Knowles** (BAH) [4]
18. P.Petzschner (GER) & A.Peya (AUT)

19. J.Tipsarevic (SRB) & V.Troicki (SRB)
20. H.Levy (ISR) & J.Thomas (USA)

21. J.Chardy (FRA) & F.Serra (FRA)
22. L.Arnold Ker (ARG) & L.Horna (PER)

23. O.Hernandez (ESP) & A.Montanes (ESP)
24. **C.Kas** (GER) & **R.Wassen** (NED) [15]

25. **J.Coetzee** (RSA) & **W.Moodie** (RSA) [11]
26. S.Bolelli (ITA) & A.Seppi (ITA)

27. F.Lopez (ESP) & F.Verdasco (ESP)
28. T.Cibulec (CZE) & I.Minar (CZE)

29. R.Haase (NED) & S.Querrey (USA)
30. F.Cipolla (ITA) & D.Gremelmayr (GER)

31. P.Hanley (AUS) & T.Perry (AUS)
32. **J.Bjorkman** (SWE) & **K.Ullyett** (ZIM) [8]

33. **M.Damm** (CZE) & **P.Vizner** (CZE) [6]
34. T.Parrott (USA) & F.Polasek (SVK)

(WC) 35. N.Bamford (GBR) & J.Goodall (GBR)
36. R.De Voest (RSA) & L.Kubot (POL)

37. E.Butorac (USA) & A.Fisher (AUS)
38. Y.Allegro (SUI) & S.Prieto (ARG)

(WC) 39. J.Auckland (GBR) & J.Delgado (GBR)
40. **L.Dlouhy** (CZE) & **L.Paes** (IND) [9]

41. **J.Benneteau** (FRA) & **N.Mahut** (FRA) [16]
42. J.Del Potro (ARG) & D.Hrbaty (SVK)

43. O.Marach (AUT) & M.Mertinak (SVK)
44. T.Johansson (SWE) & J.Melzer (AUT)

(Q) 45. KJ.Hippensteel (USA) & T.Phillips (USA)
46. S.Huss (AUS) & R.Hutchins (GBR)

47. S.Lipsky (USA) & D.Martin (USA)
48. **J.Erlich** (ISR) & **A.Ram** (ISR) [3]

49. **S.Aspelin** (SWE) & **J.Knowle** (AUT) [5]
50. K.Anderson (RSA) & R.Lindstedt (SWE)

51. S.Darcis (BEL) & K.Vliegen (BEL)
52. M.Kohlmann (GER) & J.Scherrer (SUI)

(LL) 53. J.Brunstrom (SWE) & A.Feeney (AUS)
54. C.Haggard (RSA) & L.Zovko (CRO)

(LL) 55. M.Elgin (RUS) & A.Kudryavtsev (RUS)
56. **M.Melo** (BRA) & **A.Sa** (BRA) [12]

57. **M.Mirnyi** (BLR) & **J.Murray** (GBR) [14]
58. M.Gicquel (FRA) & F.Santoro (FRA)

59. B.Soares (BRA) & D.Vemic (SRB)
60. J.Cerretani (USA) & V.Hanescu (ROU)

61. R.Ram (USA) & B.Reynolds (USA)
(Q) 62. A.Delic (USA) & B.Evans (USA)

(WC) 63. A.Bogdanovic (GBR) & J.Marray (GBR)
64. **D.Nestor** (CAN) & **N.Zimonjic** (SRB) [2]

Second Round

B.Bryan & M.Bryan [1]
7/5 6/1 6/4

I.Kunitsyn & D.Tursunov
6/3 6/2 6/2

C.Berlocq & E.Schwank
6/1 4/6 6/4 6/4

F.Cermak & J.Kerr [13]
6/4 5/7 6/4 6/4

R.Bopanna & A-U-H.Qureshi
6/3 7/5 6/4

M.Granollers & S.Ventura
7/6(2) 6/2 7/6(6)

P.Pala & I.Zelenay
7/5 6/4 6/3

F.Gil & D.Norman
7/6(3) 7/6(5) 6/3

P.Petzschner & A.Peya
7/5 6/2 7/6(4)

J.Tipsarevic & V.Troicki
6/3 6/1 6/3

L.Arnold Ker & L.Horna
6/1 6/2 6/3

C.Kas & R.Wassen [15]
7/5 6/3 6/2

J.Coetzee & W.Moodie [11]
6/1 1/6 6/3 6/2

F.Lopez & F.Verdasco
6/4 6/4 6/4

F.Cipolla & D.Gremelmayr
6/2 2/6 7/5 7/6(2)

J.Bjorkman & K.Ullyett [8]
6/4 6/4 7/5

T.Parrott & F.Polasek
6/4 7/6(6) 2/6 6/4

R.De Voest & L.Kubot
6/3 7/6(5) 6/2

E.Butorac & A.Fisher
5/7 6/4 6/4 6/7(4) 7/5

L.Dlouhy & L.Paes [9]
4/6 6/0 6/3 4/6 6/3

J.Benneteau & N.Mahut [16]
6/0 7/6(3) 6/2

T.Johansson & J.Melzer
6/2 7/5 7/5

S.Huss & R.Hutchins
6/3 6/7(5) 7/5 6/2

J.Erlich & A.Ram [3]
5/7 4/6 6/3 6/3 11/9

K.Anderson & R.Lindstedt
6/4 4/6 7/6(6) 7/6(4)

M.Kohlmann & J.Scherrer
6/4 6/2 7/6(0)

J.Brunstrom & A.Feeney
6/2 3/6 4/6 6/3 7/5

M.Melo & A.Sa [12]
6/3 3/6 4/6 6/4 6/1

M.Mirnyi & J.Murray [14]
7/6(4) 7/6(5) 6/3

J.Cerretani & V.Hanescu
6/3 3/6 7/5 7/6(3)

R.Ram & B.Reynolds
6/2 7/6(4) 6/3

D.Nestor & N.Zimonjic [2]
6/4 7/6(4) 6/1

Third Round

B.Bryan & M.Bryan [1]
6/2 6/2 6/4

F.Cermak & J.Kerr [13]
6/3 6/4 7/6(5)

M.Granollers & S.Ventura
6/2 6/4 6/2

P.Pala & I.Zelenay
4/6 2/6 6/1 7/6(4) 6/1

P.Petzschner & A.Peya
6/4 6/4 6/3

C.Kas & R.Wassen [15]
w/o

F.Lopez & F.Verdasco
7/6(2) 6/2 7/6(3)

J.Bjorkman & K.Ullyett [8]
6/4 7/6(2) 6/4

T.Parrott & F.Polasek
6/4 3/6 7/6(5) 6/4

L.Dlouhy & L.Paes [9]
6/3 7/6(3) 6/3

J.Benneteau & N.Mahut [16]
7/6(2) 6/4 6/3

J.Erlich & A.Ram [3]
6/7(3) 6/4 3/6 6/3 6/4

K.Anderson & R.Lindstedt
7/6(4) 6/4 6/2

M.Melo & A.Sa [12]
6/1 6/2 4/6 6/4

M.Mirnyi & J.Murray [14]
6/4 6/4 7/6(0)

D.Nestor & N.Zimonjic [2]
6/1 7/6(6) 2/6 7/6(1)

Quarter-Finals

B.Bryan & M.Bryan [1]
6/7(10) 6/4 6/4 6/2

M.Granollers & S.Ventura
7/5 6/2 6/4

P.Petzschner & A.Peya
6/7(5) 7/6(7) 6/2 6/4

J.Bjorkman & K.Ullyett [8]
w/o

L.Dlouhy & L.Paes [9]
7/6(2) 7/6(6) 6/4

J.Erlich & A.Ram [3]
4/6 6/7(4) 7/6(5) 6/3 6/4

K.Anderson & R.Lindstedt
w/o

D.Nestor & N.Zimonjic [2]
6/2 7/5 6/3

Semi-Finals

B.Bryan & M.Bryan [1]
7/6(3) 6/2 6/0

J.Bjorkman & K.Ullyett [8]
7/6(5) 4/6 6/3 6/7(5) 6/2

L.Dlouhy & L.Paes [9]
6/3 6/3 6/3

D.Nestor & N.Zimonjic [2]
7/6(5) 6/4 6/7(5) 6/3

Final

J.Bjorkman & K.Ullyett [8]
7/6(3) 5/7 7/6(5) 7/6(9)

D.Nestor & N.Zimonjic [2]
7/6(12) 6/7(3) 6/3 6/3

Winners

Heavy type denotes seeded players. The figure in brackets against names denotes the order in which they have been seeded. (WC)=Wild card. (Q)=Qualifier. (LL)=Lucky loser.

EVENT III – THE LADIES' SINGLES CHAMPIONSHIP 2008
HOLDER: MISS V. WILLIAMS

The Winner became the holder, for the year only, of the CHALLENGE TROPHY presented by The All England Lawn Tennis and Croquet Club in 1886. The Winner received a silver replica of the Trophy. A Silver Salver was presented to the Runner-up and a Bronze Medal to each defeated Semi-finalist. The matches were the best of three sets.

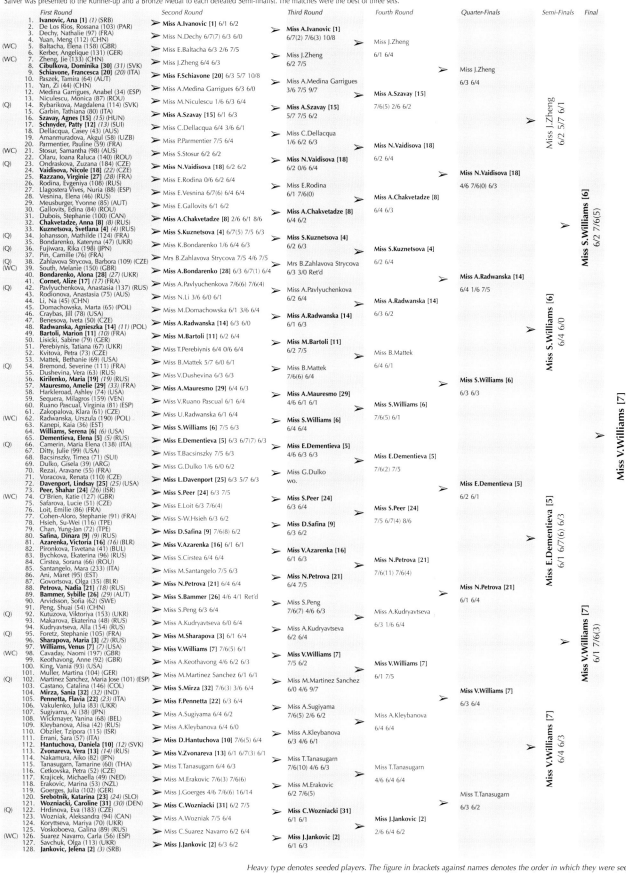

	First Round	Second Round	Third Round	Fourth Round	Quarter-Finals	Semi-Finals	Final

First Round:
1. Ivanovic, Ana [1] (1) (SRB)
2. De Los Rios, Rossana (103) (PAR)
3. Dechy, Nathalie (97) (FRA)
4. Yuan, Meng (112) (CHN)
(WC) 5. Baltacha, Elena (158) (GBR)
(WC) 6. Kerber, Angelique (131) (GER)
7. Zheng, Jie (133) (CHN)
8. Cibulkova, Dominika [30] (31) (SVK)
9. Schiavone, Francesca [20] (20) (ITA)
10. Paszek, Tamira (64) (AUT)
11. Yan, Zi (44) (CHN)
12. Medina Garrigues, Anabel (34) (ESP)
13. Niculescu, Monica (87) (ROU)
14. Rybarikova, Magdalena (114) (SVK)
15. Garbin, Tathiana (80) (ITA)
16. Szavay, Agnes [15] (15) (HUN)
17. Schnyder, Patty [12] (13) (SUI)
18. Dellacqua, Casey (43) (AUS)
19. Amanmuradova, Akgul (58) (UZB)
20. Parmentier, Pauline (59) (FRA)
(WC) 21. Stosur, Samantha (98) (AUS)
22. Olaru, Ioana Raluca (140) (ROU)
(Q) 23. Ondraskova, Zuzana (184) (CZE)
24. Vaidisova, Nicole [18] (22) (CZE)
25. Razzano, Virginie [27] (28) (FRA)
26. Rodina, Evgeniya (108) (RUS)
27. Llagostera Vives, Nuria (88) (ESP)
28. Vesnina, Elena (46) (RUS)
29. Meusburger, Yvonne (85) (AUT)
30. Gallovits, Edina (84) (ROU)
31. Dubois, Stephanie (100) (CAN)
32. Chakvetadze, Anna [8] (8) (RUS)
33. Kuznetsova, Svetlana [4] (4) (RUS)
(Q) 34. Johansson, Mathilde (124) (FRA)
35. Bondarenko, Kateryna (47) (UKR)
(Q) 36. Fujiwara, Rika (198) (JPN)
37. Pin, Camille (76) (FRA)
(Q) 38. Zahlavova Strycova, Barbora (109) (CZE)
(WC) 39. South, Melanie (150) (GBR)
40. Bondarenko, Alona [28] (27) (UKR)
41. Cornet, Alize [17] (17) (FRA)
(Q) 42. Pavlyuchenkova, Anastasia (137) (RUS)
43. Rodionova, Anastasia (75) (AUS)
44. Li, Na (45) (CHN)
45. Domachowska, Marta (65) (POL)
46. Craybas, Jill (78) (USA)
47. Benesova, Iveta (50) (CZE)
48. Radwanska, Agnieszka [14] (11) (POL)
49. Bartoli, Marion [11] (10) (FRA)
50. Lisicki, Sabine (79) (GER)
51. Perebiynis, Tatiana (67) (UKR)
52. Kvitova, Petra (73) (CZE)
53. Mattek, Bethanie (69) (USA)
(Q) 54. Bremond, Severine (111) (FRA)
55. Dushevina, Vera (63) (RUS)
56. Kirilenko, Maria [19] (19) (RUS)
57. Mauresmo, Amelie [29] (33) (FRA)
58. Harkleroad, Ashley (74) (USA)
59. Sequera, Milagros (159) (VEN)
60. Ruano Pascual, Virginia (81) (ESP)
61. Zakopalova, Klara (61) (CZE)
(WC) 62. Radwanska, Urszula (190) (POL)
63. Kanepi, Kaia (36) (EST)
64. Williams, Serena [6] (6) (USA)
65. Dementieva, Elena [5] (5) (RUS)
(Q) 66. Camerin, Maria Elena (138) (ITA)
67. Ditty, Julie (99) (USA)
68. Bacsinszky, Timea (71) (SUI)
69. Dulko, Gisela (39) (ARG)
70. Rezai, Aravane (55) (FRA)
71. Voracova, Renata (110) (CZE)
72. Davenport, Lindsay [25] (25) (USA)
73. Peer, Shahar [24] (26) (ISR)
(WC) 74. O'Brien, Katie (127) (GBR)
75. Safarova, Lucie (51) (CZE)
76. Loit, Emilie (86) (FRA)
77. Cohen-Aloro, Stephanie (91) (FRA)
78. Hsieh, Su-Wei (116) (TPE)
79. Chan, Yung-Jan (72) (TPE)
80. Safina, Dinara [9] (9) (RUS)
81. Azarenka, Victoria [16] (16) (BLR)
82. Pironkova, Tsvetana (41) (BUL)
83. Bychkova, Ekaterina (96) (RUS)
84. Cirstea, Sorana (66) (ROU)
85. Santangelo, Mara (233) (ITA)
86. Ani, Maret (95) (EST)
87. Govortsova, Olga (35) (BLR)
88. Petrova, Nadia [21] (18) (RUS)
89. Bammer, Sybille [26] (24) (AUT)
90. Arvidsson, Sofia (62) (SWE)
91. Peng, Shuai (54) (CHN)
(Q) 92. Kutuzova, Viktoriya (153) (UKR)
93. Makarova, Ekaterina (48) (RUS)
94. Kudryavtseva, Alla (154) (RUS)
(Q) 95. Foretz, Stephanie (105) (FRA)
96. Sharapova, Maria [3] (2) (RUS)
97. Williams, Venus [7] (7) (USA)
(WC) 98. Cavaday, Naomi (197) (GBR)
99. Keothavong, Anne (92) (GBR)
100. King, Vania (93) (USA)
101. Muller, Martina (104) (GER)
(Q) 102. Martinez Sanchez, Maria Jose (101) (ESP)
103. Castano, Catalina (146) (COL)
104. Mirza, Sania [32] (32) (IND)
105. Pennetta, Flavia [22] (23) (ITA)
106. Vakulenko, Julia (83) (UKR)
107. Sugiyama, Ai (38) (JPN)
108. Wickmayer, Yanina (68) (BEL)
109. Kleybanova, Alisa (42) (RUS)
110. Obziler, Tzipora (115) (ISR)
111. Errani, Sara (57) (ITA)
112. Hantuchova, Daniela [10] (12) (SVK)
113. Zvonareva, Vera [13] (14) (RUS)
114. Nakamura, Aiko (82) (JPN)
115. Tanasugarn, Tamarine (60) (THA)
116. Cetkovska, Petra (52) (CZE)
117. Krajicek, Michaella (49) (NED)
118. Erakovic, Marina (53) (NZL)
119. Goerges, Julia (102) (GER)
120. Srebotnik, Katarina [23] (24) (SLO)
121. Wozniacki, Caroline [31] (30) (DEN)
(Q) 122. Hrdinova, Eva (183) (CZE)
123. Wozniak, Aleksandra (94) (CAN)
124. Koryttseva, Mariya (70) (UKR)
125. Voskoboeva, Galina (89) (RUS)
(WC) 126. Suarez Navarro, Carla (56) (ESP)
127. Savchuk, Olga (113) (UKR)
128. Jankovic, Jelena [2] (3) (SRB)

Second Round:
Miss A.Ivanovic [1] 6/1 6/2
Miss N.Dechy 6/7(7) 6/3 6/0
Miss E.Baltacha 6/3 2/6 7/5
Miss J.Zheng 6/4 6/3
Miss F.Schiavone [20] 6/3 5/7 10/8
Miss A.Medina Garrigues 6/3 6/0
Miss M.Niculescu 6/3 6/4
Miss A.Szavay [15] 6/1 6/3
Miss C.Dellacqua 6/4 3/6 6/1
Miss P.Parmentier 7/5 6/4
Miss S.Stosur 6/2 6/2
Miss N.Vaidisova [18] 6/2 6/2
Miss E.Rodina 0/6 6/2 6/4
Miss E.Vesnina 6/7(6) 6/4 6/4
Miss E.Gallovits 6/1 6/2
Miss A.Chakvetadze [8] 2/6 6/1 8/6
Miss S.Kuznetsova [4] 6/7(5) 7/5 6/3
Miss K.Bondarenko 1/6 6/4 6/3
Mrs B.Zahlavova Strycova 7/5 4/6 7/5
Miss A.Bondarenko [28] 6/3 6/7(1) 6/4
Miss A.Pavlyuchenkova 7/6(6) 7/6(4)
Miss N.Li 3/6 6/0 6/1
Miss M.Domachowska 6/1 3/6 6/4
Miss A.Radwanska [14] 6/3 6/0
Miss M.Bartoli [11] 6/2 6/4
Miss T.Perebiynis 6/4 0/6 6/4
Miss B.Mattek 5/7 6/0 6/1
Miss V.Dushevina 6/3 6/3
Miss A.Mauresmo [29] 6/4 6/3
Miss V.Ruano Pascual 6/1 6/4
Miss U.Radwanska 6/1 6/4
Miss S.Williams [6] 7/5 6/3
Miss E.Dementieva [5] 6/3 6/7(7) 6/3
Miss T.Bacsinszky 7/5 6/3
Miss G.Dulko 1/6 6/0 6/2
Miss L.Davenport [25] 6/3 5/7 6/3
Miss S.Peer [24] 6/3 7/5
Miss E.Loit 6/3 7/6(4)
Miss S-W.Hsieh 6/3 6/2
Miss D.Safina [9] 7/6(8) 6/2
Miss V.Azarenka [16] 6/1 6/1
Miss S.Cirstea 6/4 6/4
Miss M.Santangelo 7/5 6/3
Miss N.Petrova [21] 6/4 6/4
Miss S.Bammer [26] 4/6 4/1 Ret'd
Miss S.Peng 6/3 6/4
Miss A.Kudryavtseva 6/0 6/4
Miss M.Sharapova [3] 6/1 6/4
Miss V.Williams [7] 7/6(5) 6/1
Miss A.Keothavong 4/6 6/2 6/3
Miss M.Martinez Sanchez 6/1 6/1
Miss S.Mirza [32] 7/6(3) 3/6 6/4
Miss F.Pennetta [22] 6/3 6/4
Miss A.Sugiyama 6/4 6/2
Miss A.Kleybanova 6/4 6/0
Miss D.Hantuchova [10] 7/6(5) 6/4
Miss V.Zvonareva [13] 6/1 6/7(3) 6/1
Miss T.Tanasugarn 6/4 6/3
Miss M.Erakovic 7/6(3) 7/6(6)
Miss J.Goerges 4/6 7/6(6) 16/14
Miss C.Wozniacki [31] 6/2 7/5
Miss A.Wozniak 7/5 6/4
Miss C.Suarez Navarro 6/2 6/4
Miss J.Jankovic [2] 6/3 6/2

Third Round:
Miss A.Ivanovic [1] 6/7(2) 7/6(3) 10/8
Miss J.Zheng 6/2 7/5
Miss A.Medina Garrigues 3/6 7/5 9/7
Miss A.Szavay [15] 5/7 7/5 6/2
Miss C.Dellacqua 1/6 6/2 6/3
Miss N.Vaidisova [18] 6/2 0/6 6/4
Miss E.Rodina 6/1 7/6(0)
Miss A.Chakvetadze [8] 6/4 6/2
Miss S.Kuznetsova [4] 6/2 6/3
Mrs B.Zahlavova Strycova 6/3 3/0 Ret'd
Miss A.Pavlyuchenkova 6/2 6/4
Miss A.Radwanska [14] 6/3 6/2
Miss M.Bartoli [11] 6/2 7/5
Miss B.Mattek 7/6(6) 6/4
Miss A.Mauresmo [29] 4/6 6/1 6/1
Miss S.Williams [6] 6/4 6/4
Miss E.Dementieva [5] 4/6 6/3 6/3
Miss G.Dulko wo.
Miss S.Peer [24] 6/3 6/4
Miss D.Safina [9] 6/3 6/2
Miss V.Azarenka [16] 6/1 6/3
Miss N.Petrova [21] 6/4 7/5
Miss S.Peng 7/6(7) 4/6 6/3
Miss A.Kudryavtseva 6/2 6/4
Miss M.Sharapova [3] 6/1 6/4
Miss V.Williams [7] 7/5 6/2
Miss M.Martinez Sanchez 6/0 4/6 9/7
Miss A.Sugiyama 7/6(5) 2/6 6/2
Miss A.Kleybanova 6/3 4/6 6/1
Miss T.Tanasugarn 7/6(10) 4/6 6/3
Miss M.Erakovic 6/2 7/6(5)
Miss C.Wozniacki [31] 6/1 6/1
Miss J.Jankovic [2] 6/1 6/3

Fourth Round:
Miss J.Zheng 6/1 6/4
Miss A.Szavay [15] 7/6(5) 2/6 6/2
Miss N.Vaidisova [18] 6/2 6/4
Miss S.Kuznetsova [4] 6/2 6/4
Miss A.Pavlyuchenkova 6/2 6/4
Miss A.Radwanska [14] 6/3 6/2
Miss B.Mattek 6/4 6/1
Miss S.Williams [6] 7/6(5) 6/1
Miss E.Dementieva [5] 7/6(2) 7/5
Miss S.Peer [24] 7/5 6/7(4) 8/6
Miss N.Petrova [21] 7/6(11) 7/6(4)
Miss A.Kudryavtseva 6/3 1/6 6/4
Miss V.Williams [7] 6/1 7/5
Miss A.Kleybanova 6/3 4/6 6/1
Miss T.Tanasugarn 4/6 6/4 6/4
Miss J.Jankovic [2] 2/6 6/4 6/2

Quarter-Finals:
Miss J.Zheng 6/3 6/4
Miss N.Vaidisova [18] 4/6 7/6(0) 6/3
Miss S.Kuznetsova [4] 6/2 6/3
Miss A.Radwanska [14] 6/4 1/6 7/5
Miss S.Williams [6] 6/3 6/3
Miss E.Dementieva [5] 6/2 6/1
Miss N.Petrova [21] 6/1 6/4
Miss V.Williams [7] 6/3 6/4

Semi-Finals:
Miss J.Zheng 6/2 5/7 6/1
Miss S.Williams [6] 6/4 6/0
Miss E.Dementieva [5] 6/1 6/7(6) 6/3
Miss V.Williams [7] 6/1 7/6(3)

Final:
Miss S.Williams [6] 6/2 7/6(5)
Miss V.Williams [7] 7/5 6/4

EVENT IV – THE LADIES' DOUBLES CHAMPIONSHIP 2008
HOLDERS: MISS C. BLACK & MRS L. HUBER

The Winners became the holders, for the year only, of the CHALLENGE CUPS presented by H.R.H. PRINCESS MARINA, DUCHESS OF KENT, the late President of The All England Lawn Tennis and Croquet Club in 1949 and The All England Lawn Tennis and Croquet Club in 2001. The Winners received a silver replica of the Challenge Cup. A Silver Salver was presented to each of the Runners-up and a Bronze Medal to each defeated Semi-finalist. The matches were the best of three sets.

	First Round	Second Round	Third Round	Quarter-Finals	Semi-Finals	Final	Winners
	1. **Miss C.Black** (ZIM) & **Mrs L.Huber** (USA) **[1]**						
	2. Miss N.Grandin (RSA) & Miss T.Pironkova (BUL)	Miss C.Black & Mrs L.Huber [1] 6/1 6/0					
	3. Miss V.Razzano (FRA) & Miss J.Vakulenko (UKR)		Miss C.Black & Mrs L.Huber [1] 6/0 6/2				
	4. Miss V.Dushevina (RUS) & Miss E.Dzehalevich (BLR)	Miss V.Dushevina & Miss E.Dzehalevich 6/3 6/2					
(Q)	5. Miss V.King (USA) & Miss A.Kudryavtseva (RUS)			Miss C.Black & Mrs L.Huber [1] 6/1 6/3			
	6. Miss A.Hlavackova (CZE) & Miss O.Savchuk (UKR)	Miss V.King & Miss A.Kudryavtseva 6/3 6/3					
	7. Miss M.Erakovic (NZL) & Miss M.Krajicek (NED)		Miss V.King & Miss A.Kudryavtseva 6/1 6/3				
	8. **Miss I.Benesova** (CZE) & **Miss J.Husarova** (SVK) **[15]**	Miss I.Benesova & Miss J.Husarova [15] 6/0 6/2					
	9. **Miss D.Safina** (RUS) & **Miss A.Szavay** (HUN) **[10]**				Miss C.Black & Mrs L.Huber [1] 7/5 7/6(4)		
	10. Miss T.Garbin (ITA) & Miss M.Koryttseva (UKR)	Miss D.Safina & Miss A.Szavay [10] 6/2 6/1					
	11. Miss G.Navratilova (CZE) & Mrs K.Zakopalova (CZE)		Miss D.Safina & Miss A.Szavay [10] 6/4 7/6(1)				
	12. Miss E.Loit (FRA) & Miss P.Parmentier (FRA)	Miss E.Loit & Miss P.Parmentier 7/6(1) 7/6(5)					
(LL)	13. Miss C.A.Fusano (USA) & Miss A.Haynes (USA)			Miss V.Azarenka & Miss S.Peer [6] 7/5 6/4			
	14. Miss E.Gallovits (ROU) & Miss O.Govortsova (BLR)	Miss C.A.Fusano & Miss A.Haynes 7/6(6) 6/2					
	15. Miss L.Hradecka (CZE) & Miss R.Voracova (CZE)		Miss V.Azarenka & Miss S.Peer [6] 7/6(5) 6/1				
	16. **Miss V.Azarenka** (BLR) & **Miss S.Peer** (ISR) **[6]**	Miss V.Azarenka & Miss S.Peer [6] 7/5 6/4					
	17. **Mrs K.Peschke** (CZE) & **Miss R.P.Stubbs** (AUS) **[3]**						
	18. Miss S.Bammer (AUT) & Miss M.Muller (GER)	Mrs K.Peschke & Miss R.P.Stubbs [3] 6/2 6/2					
	19. Miss D.Cibulkova (SVK) & Miss A.Kleybanova (RUS)		Mrs K.Peschke & Miss R.P.Stubbs [3] 6/1 6/2				
	20. Miss S.Cirstea (ROU) & Miss M.Niculescu (ROU)	Miss S.Cirstea & Miss M.Niculescu 6/1 0/0 Ret'd					
	21. Miss S-W.Hsieh (TPE) & Miss M.Washington (USA)			Miss L.M.Raymond & Miss S.Stosur [16] 6/2 7/6(3)			
	22. Miss Y.Shvedova (RUS) & Miss T.Tanasugarn (THA)	Miss Y.Shvedova & Miss T.Tanasugarn 6/1 6/2					
	23. Miss A.Harkleroad (USA) & Miss G.Voskoboeva (RUS)		Miss L.M.Raymond & Miss S.Stosur [16] 7/5 6/7(7) 6/4				
	24. **Miss L.M.Raymond** (USA) & **Miss S.Stosur** (AUS) **[16]**	Miss L.M.Raymond & Miss S.Stosur [16] 3/6 6/2 6/1					
	25. **Miss Z.Yan** (CHN) & **Miss J.Zheng** (CHN) **[9]**				Miss L.M.Raymond & Miss S.Stosur [16] 6/4 6/3		
	26. Miss A.Parra Santonja (ESP) & Miss C.Suarez Navarro (ESP)	Miss Z.Yan & Miss J.Zheng [9] 6/4 6/2					
	27. Miss E.Hrdinova (CZE) & Miss P.Kvitova (CZE)		Miss Z.Yan & Miss J.Zheng [9] 6/3 6/2				
	28. Miss E.Vesnina (RUS) & Miss V.Zvonareva (RUS)	Miss E.Vesnina & Miss V.Zvonareva 7/6(8) 4/6 6/2					
	29. Miss P.Cetkovska (CZE) & Miss L.Safarova (CZE)			Miss E.Makarova & Miss S.Sfar 7/5 6/4			
	30. Miss M.E.Camerin (ITA) & Miss G.Dulko (ARG)	Miss M.E.Camerin & Miss G.Dulko 6/3 6/2					
	31. Miss E.Makarova (RUS) & Miss S.Sfar (TUN)		Miss E.Makarova & Miss S.Sfar 6/3 6/0				
(LL)	32. Miss A.Morita (JPN) & Miss J.Namigata (JPN)	Miss E.Makarova & Miss S.Sfar 6/3 6/3					
	33. **Miss A.Medina Garrigues** (ESP) & **Miss V.Ruano Pascual** (ESP) **[5]**						
	34. Miss S.Foretz (FRA) & Miss C.Pin (FRA)	Miss A.Medina Garrigues & Miss V.Ruano Pascual [5] 6/3 6/1					
	35. Miss T.Paszek (AUT) & Miss J.Woehr (GER)		Miss A.Medina Garrigues & Miss V.Ruano Pascual [5] 6/1 6/3				
	36. Miss S.Errani (ITA) & Miss F.Schiavone (ITA)	Miss S.Errani & Miss F.Schiavone 7/5 7/6(6)					
(WC)	37. Miss S.Borwell (GBR) & Miss J.Rae (GBR)			Miss S.Williams & Miss V.Williams [11] 6/1 6/4			
(POL)	38. Miss M.Domachowska (POL) & Miss A.Radwanska	Miss M.Domachowska & Miss A.Radwanska 6/3 6/4					
	39. Miss T.Poutchek (BLR) & Miss A.Rodionova (AUS)		Miss S.Williams & Miss V.Williams [11] 6/0 6/4				
	40. **Miss S.Williams** (USA) & **Miss V.Williams** (USA) **[11]**	Miss S.Williams & Miss V.Williams [11] 6/0 6/3					
	41. **Miss B.Mattek** (USA) & **Miss S.Mirza** (IND) **[13]**				Miss S.Williams & Miss V.Williams [11] 6/4 6/3		
(WC)	42. Miss E.Baltacha (GBR) & Miss N.Cavaday (GBR)	Miss B.Mattek & Miss S.Mirza [13] 6/4 6/2					
	43. Miss J.Craybas (USA) & Miss C.Wozniacki (DEN)		Miss B.Mattek & Miss S.Mirza [13] 6/3 6/4				
(Q)	44. Miss M.Kirilenko (RUS) & Miss F.Pennetta (ITA)	Miss M.Kirilenko & Miss F.Pennetta 6/1 6/3					
(WC)	45. Miss A.Keothavong (GBR) & Miss M.South (GBR)			Miss B.Mattek & Miss S.Mirza [13] 4/6 6/4 2/0 Ret'd			
	46. Miss C.Ji (CHN) & Miss S-N.Sun (CHN)	Miss A.Keothavong & Miss M.South 7/6(5) 6/4					
	47. Miss A.Amanmuradova (UZB) & Miss D.Kustova (BLR)		Miss A.Amanmuradova & Miss D.Kustova 6/4 4/6 7/5				
	48. **Miss Y-J.Chan** (TPE) & **Miss C.Chuang** (TPE) **[4]**	Miss A.Amanmuradova & Miss D.Kustova 4/6 7/6(3) 6/3					
	49. **Miss S.Peng** (CHN) & **Miss T.Sun** (CHN) **[8]**				Miss N.Llagostera Vives & Miss M.Martinez Sanchez 6/4 6/4		
	50. Miss C.Castano (COL) & Miss K.Kanepi (EST)	Miss C.Castano & Miss K.Kanepi 2/6 6/4 9/7					
	51. Miss K.Jans (POL) & Miss M.Jugic-Salkic (BIH)		Miss C.Castano & Miss K.Kanepi 7/5 6/4				
	52. Miss C.Gullickson (USA) & Miss V.Uhlirova (CZE)	Miss C.Gullickson & Miss V.Uhlirova 6/3 4/6 7/5					
	53. Miss A.Nakamura (JPN) & Miss A.Rezai (FRA)			Miss N.Llagostera Vives & Miss M.Martinez Sanchez 6/2 7/5			
(WC)	54. Miss A.Elliott (GBR) & Miss K.O'Brien (GBR)	Miss A.Nakamura & Miss A.Rezai 7/5 6/4					
	55. Miss N.Llagostera Vives (ESP) & Miss M.Martinez Sanchez (ESP)		Miss N.Llagostera Vives & Miss M.Martinez Sanchez 6/2 7/5				
(LL)	56. Miss A.Smith (GBR) & Miss G.Stoop (GBR)	Miss N.Llagostera Vives & Miss M.Martinez Sanchez 7/6(7) 7/6(3)					
	57. **Miss A.Molik** (AUS) & **Miss M.Santangelo** (ITA) **[14]**				Miss N.Dechy & Miss C.Dellacqua 6/3 6/2		
	58. Miss T.Perebiynis (UKR) & Miss A.Rosolska (POL)	Miss T.Perebiynis & Miss A.Rosolska 7/5 7/6(2) 6/4					
(WC)	59. Miss A.Fitzpatrick (GBR) & Miss A.Hawkins (GBR)		Miss N.Dechy & Miss C.Dellacqua 6/3 6/2				
	60. Miss N.Dechy (FRA) & Miss C.Dellacqua (AUS)	Miss N.Dechy & Miss C.Dellacqua 6/1 6/0					
	61. Miss T.Bacsinszky (SUI) & Miss A.Cornet (FRA)			Miss N.Dechy & Miss C.Dellacqua 6/3 7/6(9)			
(Q)	62. Miss R.Kops-Jones (USA) & Miss A.Spears (USA)	Miss R.Kops-Jones & Miss A.Spears 3/6 7/5 6/2					
(Q)	63. Miss J.Cravero (ARG) & Miss B.Jozami (ARG)		Miss R.Kops-Jones & Miss A.Spears 2/6 6/3 11/9				
	64. **Miss A.Sugiyama** (JPN) & **Miss K.Srebotnik** (SLO) **[2]**	Miss A.Sugiyama & Miss K.Srebotnik [2] 6/4 6/0					

Quarter-Finals / Semi-Finals additional results:

- Miss V.Azarenka & Miss S.Peer [6]
- Miss C.Black & Mrs L.Huber [1] 7/5 7/6(4)
- Miss L.M.Raymond & Miss S.Stosur [16] 6/4 6/3
- Miss S.Williams & Miss V.Williams [11] 6/4 6/3
- Miss N.Dechy & Miss C.Dellacqua 6/2 6/7(6) 6/4

Semi-Finals:
- Miss C.Black & Mrs L.Huber [1] 7/5 7/6(4)
- Miss L.M.Raymond & Miss S.Stosur [16] 6/3 6/3
- Miss S.Williams & Miss V.Williams [11] 6/3 6/3

Final:
- Miss L.M.Raymond & Miss S.Stosur [16] 6/3 6/3
- Miss S.Williams & Miss V.Williams [11] 6/3 6/3

Winners:
- **Miss S.Williams & Miss V.Williams [11]** 6/2 6/2

Heavy type denotes seeded players. The figure in brackets against names denotes the order in which they were seeded. (WC)=Wild card. (Q)=Qualifier. (LL)=Lucky loser.

EVENT V – THE MIXED DOUBLES CHAMPIONSHIP 2008
HOLDERS: J. MURRAY & MISS J. JANKOVIC

The Winners became the holders, for the year only, of the CHALLENGE CUPS presented by members of the family of the late Mr. S. H. SMITH in 1949 and The All England Lawn Tennis and Croquet Club in 2001. The Winners received a silver replica of the Challenge Cup. A Silver Salver was presented to each of the Runners-up and a Bronze Medal to each defeated Semi-finalist. The matches were the best of three sets.

First Round

1. **M.Bryan** (USA) & **Miss K.Srebotnik** (SLO) [1]
2. Bye
3. B.Soares (BRA) & Miss M.Martinez Sanchez (ESP)
4. M.Matkowski (POL) & Miss C.Wozniacki (DEN)
5. A.Calleri (ARG) & Miss K.Kanepi (EST)
(WC) 6. R.Bloomfield (GBR) & Miss S.Borwell (GBR)
7. Bye
8. **M.Damm** (CZE) & **Miss S.Peng** (CHN) [14]
9. **L.Paes** (IND) & **Miss R.P.Stubbs** (AUS) [10]
10. Bye
11. J.Bjorkman (SWE) & Miss A.Molik (AUS)
12. F.Cermak (CZE) & Miss L.Hradecka (CZE)
13. D.Vemic (SRB) & Miss F.Pennetta (ITA)
14. S.Ratiwatana (THA) & Miss N.Llagostera Vives (ESP)
15. Bye
16. **K.Ullyett** (ZIM) & **Miss A.Sugiyama** (JPN) [5]
17. **P.Vizner** (CZE) & **Mrs K.Peschke** (CZE) [3]
18. Bye
(WC) 19. J.Auckland (GBR) & Miss E.Baltacha (GBR)
20. D.Skoch (CZE) & Miss I.Benesova (CZE)
21. I.Kunitsyn (RUS) & Miss E.Vesnina (RUS)
22. R.Bopanna (IND) & Miss T.Poutchek (BLR)
23. Bye
24. **S.Aspelin** (SWE) & **Miss L.M.Raymond** (USA) [13]
25. **M.Bhupathi** (IND) & **Miss S.Mirza** (IND) [11]
26. Bye
27. I.Andreev (RUS) & Miss M.Kirilenko (RUS)
(A) 28. S.Ratiwatana (THA) & Miss A.Kleybanova (RUS)
29. M.Melo (BRA) & Miss A.Cornet (FRA)
30. Ł.Dlouhy (CZE) & Miss N.Vaidisova (CZE)
31. Bye
32. **N.Zimonjic** (SRB) & **Miss T.Sun** (CHN) [8]
33. **M.Knowles** (BAH) & **Miss Z.Yan** (CHN) [7]
34. Bye
35. S.Lipsky (USA) & Miss C.Dellacqua (AUS)
36. F.Verdasco (ESP) & Miss M.Domachowska (POL)
37. R.Wassen (NED) & Miss V.Razzano (FRA)
(WC) 38. J.Delgado (GBR) & Miss K.O'Brien (GBR)
39. Bye
40. **A.Ram** (ISR) & **Miss N.Dechy** (FRA) [9]
41. **J.Kerr** (AUS) & **Miss K.Bondarenko** (UKR) [16]
42. Bye
43. B.Bryan (USA) & Miss S.Stosur (AUS)
44. E.Butorac (USA) & Miss B.Mattek (USA)
(WC) 45. A.Bogdanovic (GBR) & Miss M.South (GBR)
46. Y.Allegro (SUI) & Miss A.Szavay (HUN)
47. Bye
48. **P.Hanley** (AUS) & **Miss C.Black** (ZIM) [4]
49. **J.Knowle** (AUT) & **Miss Y-J.Chan** (TPE) [6]
50. Bye
(WC) 51. R.Hutchins (GBR) & Miss A.Keothavong (GBR)
52. T.Perry (AUS) & Miss M.Santangelo (ITA)
53. D.Martin (USA) & Miss V.King (USA)
54. D.Tursunov (RUS) & Miss N.Petrova (RUS)
55. Bye
56. **J.Murray** (GBR) & **Mrs L.Huber** (USA) [12]
57. **J.Coetzee** (RSA) & **Miss V.Uhlirova** (CZE) [15]
58. Bye
59. R.Lindstedt (SWE) & Miss A.Rodionova (AUS)
60. M.Mirnyi (BLR) & Miss O.Govortsova (BLR)
61. A.Sa (BRA) & Miss J.Husarova (SVK)
62. W.Moodie (RSA) & Miss J.Craybas (USA)
63. Bye
64. **D.Nestor** (CAN) & **Miss C.Chuang** (TPE) [2]

Second Round

- M.Bryan & Miss K.Srebotnik [1]
- M.Matkowski & Miss C.Wozniacki — 6/7(5) 6/2 6/3
- A.Calleri & Miss K.Kanepi — 6/4 6/2
- M.Damm & S.Peng [14]
- L.Paes & Miss R.P.Stubbs [10]
- J.Bjorkman & Miss A.Molik — 4/6 6/3 6/1
- D.Vemic & Miss F.Pennetta — 6/3 6/2
- K.Ullyett & Miss A.Sugiyama [5]
- P.Vizner & Mrs K.Peschke [3]
- D.Skoch & Miss I.Benesova — 6/7(3) 7/6(4) 9/7
- R.Bopanna & Miss T.Poutchek — 6/4 2/6 6/4
- S.Aspelin & Miss L.M.Raymond [13]
- M.Bhupathi & Miss S.Mirza [11]
- I.Andreev & Miss M.Kirilenko — 4/6 6/1 7/5
- L.Dlouhy & Miss N.Vaidisova — 5/7 6/4 6/2
- N.Zimonjic & Miss T.Sun [8]
- M.Knowles & Miss Z.Yan [7]
- S.Lipsky & Miss C.Dellacqua — 4/6 6/3 7/5
- J.Delgado & Miss K.O'Brien — 4/6 6/3 6/2
- A.Ram & Miss N.Dechy [9]
- J.Kerr & Miss K.Bondarenko [16]
- B.Bryan & Miss S.Stosur — 6/7(5) 6/1 6/3
- Y.Allegro & Miss A.Szavay — 7/6(6) 2/6 9/7
- P.Hanley & Miss C.Black [4]
- J.Knowle & Y-J.Chan [6]
- R.Hutchins & Miss A.Keothavong — 5/7 6/1 6/4
- D.Tursunov & Miss N.Petrova — 6/4 6/2
- J.Murray & Mrs L.Huber [12]
- J.Coetzee & Miss V.Uhlirova [15]
- M.Mirnyi & Miss O.Govortsova — 4/6 7/5 6/1
- W.Moodie & Miss J.Craybas — 6/2 6/2
- D.Nestor & Miss C.Chuang [2]

Third Round

- M.Bryan & Miss K.Srebotnik [1] — 6/3 6/2
- M.Damm & Miss S.Peng [14] — w/o
- J.Bjorkman & Miss A.Molik — 6/3 3/6 6/3
- K.Ullyett & Miss A.Sugiyama [5] — 2/6 7/5 7/5
- P.Vizner & Mrs K.Peschke [3] — 6/1 7/6(3)
- S.Aspelin & Miss L.M.Raymond [13] — 6/3 7/6(1)
- I.Andreev & Miss M.Kirilenko — 7/6(4) 6/3
- L.Dlouhy & Miss N.Vaidisova — 7/5 7/5
- S.Lipsky & Miss C.Dellacqua — 6/3 3/6 6/4
- A.Ram & Miss N.Dechy [9] — 6/4 6/0
- B.Bryan & Miss S.Stosur — 6/0 7/5
- P.Hanley & Miss C.Black [4] — 6/4 6/4
- J.Knowle & Miss Y-J.Chan [6] — 6/4 6/4
- J.Murray & Mrs L.Huber [12] — 6/2 2/6 9/7
- M.Mirnyi & Miss O.Govortsova — 4/6 6/4 6/1
- D.Nestor & Miss C.Chuang [2] — 7/6(5) 6/2

Quarter-Finals

- M.Bryan & Miss K.Srebotnik [1] — 7/6(4) 6/2
- K.Ullyett & Miss A.Sugiyama [5] — 6/7(5) 6/2 6/2
- P.Vizner & Mrs K.Peschke [3] — w/o
- I.Andreev & Miss M.Kirilenko — w/o
- A.Ram & Miss N.Dechy [9] — 6/3 7/5
- B.Bryan & Miss S.Stosur — 6/4 4/6 6/1
- J.Murray & Mrs L.Huber [12] — 6/4 6/3
- D.Nestor & Miss C.Chuang [2] — 6/3 7/6(4)

Semi-Finals

- M.Bryan & Miss K.Srebotnik [1] — 6/4 6/2
- I.Andreev & Miss M.Kirilenko — 6/3 6/4
- B.Bryan & Miss S.Stosur — 6/4 6/2
- J.Murray & Mrs L.Huber [12] — 6/4 7/5

Final

- M.Bryan & Miss K.Srebotnik [1] — 6/3 3/6 6/3
- B.Bryan & Miss S.Stosur — 2/6 7/6(1) 6/4

Winners

B.Bryan & Miss S. Stosur — 7/5 6/4

Heavy type denotes seeded players. The figure in brackets against names denotes the order in which they were seeded. (WC)=Wild card. (A)=Alternates.

EVENT VI – THE GENTLEMEN'S INVITATION DOUBLES 2008
HOLDERS: J. ELTINGH & P. HAARHUIS

The Winners became the holders, for the year only, of a cup presented by The All England Lawn Tennis and Croquet Club. The Winners received miniature silver salvers. A silver medal was presented to each of the Runners-up. The matches were the best of three sets. If a match reached one set all a 10 point tie-break replaced the third set.

GROUP A	P. Cash (AUS) & Ferreira W. (RSA)	Eltingh J. (NED) & Haarhuis P. (NED)	Middleton T.J. (USA) & Wheaton D. (USA)	Petchey M. (GBR) & Wilkinson C. (GBR)	WINS	LOSSES
P. Cash (AUS) & Ferreira W. (RSA)		5-7 3-6 L	7-5 6-7(5) [11-13] L	7-6(3) 7-6(4) W	1	2
Eltingh J. (NED) & Haarhuis P. (NED)	7-5 6-3 W		6-4 6-1 W	4-6 6-3 [10-4] W	3	0
Middleton T.J. (USA) & Wheaton D. (USA)	5-7 7-6(5) [13-11] W	4-6 1-6 L		4-6 4-6 L	1	2
Petchey M. (GBR) & Wilkinson C. (GBR)	6-7(3) 6-7(4) L	6-4 3-6 [4-10] L	6-4 6-4 W		1	2

GROUP B	Forget G. (FRA) & Pioline C. (FRA)	Jensen L. (USA) & Jensen M. (USA)	Johnson D. (USA) & Palmer J. (USA)	Woodbridge T.A. (AUS) & Woodforde M. (AUS)	WINS	LOSSES
Forget G. (FRA) & Pioline C. (FRA)		6-4 6-2 W	3-6 3-6 L	6-7(3) 3-6 L	1	2
Jensen L. (USA) & Jensen M. (USA)	4-6 2-6 L		2-6 4-6 L	6-7(2) 2-6 L	0	3
Johnson D. (USA) & Palmer J. (USA)	6-3 6-3 W	6-2 6-4 W		6-3 7-6(4) W	3	0
Woodbridge T.A. (AUS) & Woodforde M. (AUS)	7-6(3) 6-3 W	7-6(2) 6-2 W	3-6 6-7(4) L		2	1

FINAL

Eltingh J. (NED) & Haarhuis P. (NED)
Johnson D. (USA) & Palmer J. (USA) — Walkover

Winner: Johnson D. (USA) & Palmer J. (USA) Walkover

This event was played on a 'round robin' basis. 8 invited pairs were divided into 2 groups and each pair in each group played one another.
The pairs winning most matches were the winners of their respective groups and played a final round as indicated above.
If matches were equal in any group, the head to head result between the two pairs with the same number of wins, determined the winning pair of the group.
If that did not split the ties, then the percentage of sets won to sets played decided.

EVENT VII – THE GENTLEMEN'S SENIOR INVITATION DOUBLES 2008
HOLDERS: HOLDERS: M.J. BATES & A. JARRYD

The Winners became the holders, for the year only, of a Cup presented by The All England Lawn Tennis and Croquet Club. The Winners received miniature silver salvers. A Silver Medal was presented to each of the Runners-up. The matches were the best of three sets. If a match reached one set all a 10 point tie-break replaced the third set.

GROUP A	Amritraj V. (IND) & Mayer G. (USA)	Bahrami M. (IRI) & Leconte H. (FRA)	Bates M.J. (GBR) & Jarryd A. (SWE)	Guenthardt H. (SUI) & Taroczy B. (HUN)	WINS	LOSSES
Amritraj V. (IND) & Mayer G. (USA)		0-6 2-6 W	3-6 3-6 L	7-6(4) 6-1 W	2	1
Bahrami M. (IRI) & Leconte H. (FRA)	6-0 6-2 L		6-1 7-6(4) L	6-4 6-2 W	1	2
Bates M.J. (GBR) & Jarryd A. (SWE)	6-3 6-3 W	1-6 6-7(4) W		6-1 6-1 W	3	0
Guenthardt H. (SUI) & Taroczy B. (HUN)	6-7(4) 1-6 L	4-6 2-6 L	1-6 1-6 L		0	3

GROUP B	Curren K. (USA) & Fitzgerald J.B. (AUS)	Flach K. (USA) & Seguso R. (USA)	Fleming P. (USA) & Vilas G. (ARG)	McNamara P. (AUS) & McNamee P.F. (AUS)	WINS	LOSSES
Curren K. (USA) & Fitzgerald J.B. (AUS)		W-O L	6-3 5-5 Ret'd L	W-O L	0	3
Flach K. (USA) & Seguso R. (USA)	W-O W		6-0 6-1 W	4-6 6-3 [10-7] W	3	0
Fleming P. (USA) & Vilas G. (ARG)	3-6 5-5 Ret'd W	0-6 1-6 L		1-6 3-6 L	1	2
McNamara P. (AUS) & McNamee P.F. (AUS)	W-O W	6-4 3-6 [7-10] L	6-1 6-3 W		2	1

FINAL

Bates M.J. (GBR) & Jarryd A. (SWE)
Flach K. (USA) & Seguso R. (USA)

Winner: Flach K. (USA) & Seguso R. (USA) 7-6(1) 6-7(5) [10/7]

This event was played on a 'round robin' basis. 8 invited pairs were divided into 2 groups and each pair in each group played one another.
The pairs winning most matches were the winners of their respective groups and played a final round as indicated above.
If matches were equal in any group, the head to head result between the two pairs with the same number of wins, determined the winning pair of the group.
If that did not split the ties, then the percentage of sets won to sets played decided.

EVENT VIII – THE LADIES' INVITATION DOUBLES 2008
HOLDERS: MISS J. NOVOTNA & MISS H. SUKOVA

The Winners became the holders, for the year only, of a Cup presented by The All England Lawn Tennis and Croquet Club. The Winners received miniature Cups. A Silver Medal was presented to each of the Runners-up. The matches were the best of three sets. If a match reached one set all a 10 point tie-break replaced the third set.

GROUP A	Miss S. Appelmans (BEL) & Miss H. Mandlikova (AUS)	Miss I. Kloss (RSA) & Mrs R.D. Nideffer (USA)	Miss J. Novotna (CZE) & Mrs K. Rinaldi (USA)	Mrs E.M. Smylie (AUS) & Miss N. Tauziat (FRA)	WINS	LOSSES	FINAL
Miss S. Appelmans (BEL) & Miss H. Mandlikova (AUS)		6-7(4) 7-6(1) [9-11] L	0-6 1-6 L	4-6 3-6 L	0	3	
Mrs C. Bassett-Seguso (CAN) & Miss M.M. Bollegraf (NED)	7-6(4) 6-7(1) [11-9] W		W-O L	1-6 3-6 L	1	2	
Miss J. Novotna (CZE) & Mrs K. Rinaldi (USA)	6-0 6-1 W	W-O W		6-4 6-1 W	3	0	
Mrs E.M. Smylie (AUS) & Miss N. Tauziat (FRA)	6-4 6-3 W	6-1 6-3 W	4-6 1-6 L		2	1	

Final: Miss J. Novotna (CZE) & Mrs K. Rinaldi (USA)

GROUP B	Miss A. Croft (GBR) & Miss J.M. Durie (GBR)	Miss I. Kloss (RSA) & Mrs R.D. Nideffer (USA)	Mrs G. Magers (USA) & Miss C. Martinez (ESP)	Miss M. Navratilova (USA) & Miss H. Sukova (CZE)	WINS	LOSSES	FINAL
Miss A. Croft (GBR) & Miss J.M. Durie (GBR)		3-6 0-6 L	W-O L	1-6 0-1 Ret'd L	0	3	
Miss I. Kloss (RSA) & Mrs R.D. Nideffer (USA)	6-3 6-0 W		3-6 1-6 L	4-6 6-4 [4-10] L	1	2	
Mrs G. Magers (USA) & Miss C. Martinez (ESP)	W-O W	6-3 6-1 W		4-6 3-6 L	2	1	
Miss M. Navratilova (USA) & Miss H. Sukova (CZE)	6-1 1-0 Ret'd W	6-4 4-6 [10-4] W	6-4 6-3 W		3	0	

Final: Miss M. Navratilova (USA) & Miss H. Sukova (CZE)

Winner: Miss J. Novotna (CZE) & Miss H. Sukova (CZE) 5-7 6-3 [10/5]

This event was played on a 'round robin' basis. 8 invited pairs were divided into 2 groups of 4 and each pair in each group played one another.
The pairs winning most matches were the winners of their respective groups and played a final round as indicated above.
If matches were equal in any group, the head to head result between the two pairs with the same number of wins, determined the winning pair of the group.
If that did not split the ties, then the percentage of sets won to sets played decided.

EVENT IX – THE WHEELCHAIR GENTLEMEN'S DOUBLES 2008
HOLDERS: R. AMMERLAAN & R. VINK

The Winners received Silver Salvers. The matches were the best of three tie-break sets.

Third & Fourth Place Play-off	First Round	Final	
	1. R.Ammerlaan (NED) & R.Vink (NED) [1]	**R.Ammerlaan (NED) & R.Vink (NED) [1]** 6-0 6-2	**R.Ammerlaan (NED) & R.Vink (NED) [2]** 6-7(6) 6-1 6-3
D.Phillipson (GBR) & G.Reid (GBR)	2. D.Phillipson (GBR) & G.Reid (GBR)		
T.Kruszelnicki (POL) & M.Legner (AUT) 6-4 6-2	3. T.Kruszelnicki (POL) & M.Legner (AUT)	S.Houdet (FRA) & N.Peifer (FRA) [2] 6-2 6-3	
T.Kruszelnicki (POL) & M.Legner (AUT)	**4. S.Houdet (FRA) & N.Peifer (FRA) [2]**		

Heavy type denoted seeded players. The figure in brackets against names denoted the order in which they were seeded.

ALPHABETICAL LIST – INVITATION DOUBLES EVENTS
GENTLEMEN

Cash P. *(Australia)*
Eltingh J. *(Netherlands)*
Ferreira W. *(South Africa)*
Forget G. *(France)*

Haarhuis P. *(Netherlands)*
Jensen L. *(USA)*
Jensen M. *(USA)*
Johnson D. *(USA)*

Middleton T.J. *(USA)*
Palmer J. *(USA)*
Petchey M. *(Great Britain)*
Pioline C. *(France)*

Wheaton D. *(USA)*
Wilkinson C. *(Great Britain)*
Woodbridge T.A. *(Australia)*
Woodforde M. *(Australia)*

LADIES

Appelmans Miss S. *(Belgium)*
Bassett-Seguso Mrs C. *(Canada)*
Bollegraf Miss M.M. *(Netherlands)*
Croft Miss A. *(Great Britain)*

Durie Miss J.M. *(Great Britain)*
Kloss Miss I. *(South Africa)*
Magers Mrs G. *(USA)*
Mandlikova Miss H. *(Australia)*

Martinez Miss C. *(Spain)*
Navratilova Miss M. *(USA)*
Nideffer Mrs R.D. *(USA)*
Novotna Miss J. *(Czech Republic)*

Rinaldi Mrs K. *(USA)*
Smylie Mrs E.M. *(Australia)*
Sukova Miss H. *(Czech Republic)*
Tauziat Miss N. *(France)*

ALPHABETICAL LIST – GENTLEMEN'S SENIOR INVITATION DOUBLES EVENT

Amritraj V. *(India)*
Bahrami M. *(Iran)*
Bates M.J. *(Great Britain)*
Curren K. *(USA)*

Fitzgerald J.B. *(Australia)*
Flach K. *(USA)*
Fleming P. *(USA)*
Guenthardt H. *(Switzerland)*

Jarryd A. *(Sweden)*
Leconte H. *(France)*
Mayer G. *(USA)*
McNamara P. *(Australia)*

McNamee P.F. *(Australia)*
Seguso R. *(USA)*
Taroczy B. *(Hungary)*
Vilas G. *(Argentina)*

EVENT X – THE BOYS' SINGLES CHAMPIONSHIP 2008
HOLDER: D. YOUNG

The Winner became the holder, for the year only, of a Cup presented by The All England Lawn Tennis and Croquet Club. The Winner received a miniature Cup and the Runner-up received a memento. The matches were best of three sets.

First Round	Second Round	Third Round	Quarter-Finals	Semi-Finals	Final	Winner
1. **Tomic, Bernard [1]** (AUS)	B.Tomic [1] 6/2 6/1	B.Tomic [1] 2/6 6/1 6/4	B.Tomic [1] 6/3 5/7 6/4	B.Tomic [1] 4/6 6/4 6/3	H.Kontinen 7/6(3) 6/4	G.Dimitrov [9] 7/5 6/3
(WC) 2. Boluda-Purkiss, Carlos (ESP)						
3. Rungkat, Christopher (INA)	C.Rungkat 3/6 7/5 6/1					
(WC) 4. Marsalek, James (GBR)						
(Q) 5. Britton, Devin (USA)	H.Ehara 6/3 6/7(2) 6/4	M.Willis [15] 6/4 6/2				
(Q) 6. Ehara, Hiroyasu (JPN)						
7. Miccini, Giacomo (ITA)	M.Willis [15] 6/3 3/6 11/9					
8. **Willis, Marcus [15]** (GBR)						
9. **Grigorov, Alexei [11]** (RUS)	A.Grigorov [11] 6/2 3/6 6/3	P.Lang 6/3 6/4	H.Cunha [6] 6/2 6/2			
10. Garanganga, Takanyi (ZIM)						
(WC) 11. Pauffley, Neil (GBR)	P.Lang 6/3 6/4					
(Q) 12. Lang, Philipp (AUT)						
(Q) 13. Raonic, Milos (CAN)	M.Raonic 6/4 7/6(5)	H.Cunha [6] 6/4 6/4				
(WC) 14. Chaudry, James (GBR)						
15. Jenkins, Jarmere (USA)	H.Cunha [6] 6/2 6/3					
16. **Cunha, Henrique [6]** (BRA)						
17. **Janowicz, Jerzy [4]** (POL)	J.Janowicz [4] 4/6 6/2 6/2	Z.Zhang 4/6 6/4 6/3	H.Kontinen 6/2 3/6 8/6	H.Kontinen 6/2 6/2		
(WC) 18. James, Mathew (GBR)						
(WC) 19. Knights, Thomas (GBR)	Z.Zhang 6/4 6/4					
20. Zhang, Ze (CHN)						
21. Kontinen, Henri (FIN)	H.Kontinen 7/6(5) 7/6(3)	H.Kontinen 6/4 6/2				
22. Folie, Alexandre (BEL)						
23. Longhi, Tadayuki (JPN)	C.Buchanan [14] 6/3 7/6(7)					
24. **Buchanan, Chase [14]** (USA)						
25. **Siributwong, Peerakit [12]** (THA)	D.Evans 7/6(4) 4/6 6/2	D.Evans 7/6(8) 1/6 6/4	D.Propoggia 7/6(5) 6/4			
26. Evans, Daniel (GBR)						
(Q) 27. Crepaldi, Erik (ITA)	G.Rufin 6/4 6/1					
28. Rufin, Guillaume (FRA)						
(Q) 29. Propoggia, Dane (AUS)	D.Propoggia 6/4 3/6 11/9	D.Propoggia 4/6 6/4 6/1				
30. Puc, Borut (SLO)						
31. Basic, Mirza (BIH)	M.Basic 6/4 6/1					
32. **Arevalo, Marcelo [8]** (ESA)						
33. **Bhambri, Yuki [5]** (IND)	T.D.Trombetta 7/6(2) 6/4	T.D.Trombetta 7/6(1) 6/3	G.Dimitrov [9] 6/0 6/1	G.Dimitrov [9] 6/3 7/5	G.Dimitrov [9] 6/3 6/3	
34. Trombetta, Ty D (USA)						
35. Spong, Xander (NED)	M.Verryth 6/2 6/3					
36. Verryth, Mark (AUS)						
37. Angus, Niall (GBR)	N.Angus 6/4 4/6 6/4	G.Dimitrov [9] 7/6(3) 6/4				
38. Saavedra-Corvalan, Cristobal (CHI)						
(Q) 39. Rola, Blaz (SLO)	G.Dimitrov [9] 7/6(6) 6/3					
40. **Dimitrov, Grigor [9]** (BUL)						
41. **Klahn, Bradley [16]** (USA)	B.Klahn 6/4 6/7(7) 6/0	B.Klahn [16] 7/6(4) 6/4	C.Ramirez [3] 7/6(1) 6/2			
42. Wu, Di (CHN)						
43. Papasidero, Lorenzo (ITA)	D.Smethurst 6/3 6/3					
44. Smethurst, Daniel (GBR)						
45. Spir, Juan-Carlos (COL)	J-C.Spir 6/4 7/6(3) 6/2	C.Ramirez [3] 6/2 6/2				
(LL) 46. Moser, Niki (AUT)						
47. Reid, Matt (AUS)	C.Ramirez [3] 6/3 6/3					
48. **Ramirez, Cesar [3]** (MEX)						
49. **Harrison, Ryan [7]** (USA)	R.Harrison 6/7(5) 7/6(8) 6/4	F.Krajinovic 7/5 6/3	F.Krajinovic 6/1 6/2	F.Krajinovic 7/6(2) 6/4		
50. Pospisil, Vasek (CAN)						
51. Draganja, Marin (CRO)	F.Krajinovic 6/4 6/4					
(Q) 52. Krajinovic, Filip (SRB)						
53. Moriya, Hiroki (JPN)	J.Easton 6/4 4/6 6/4	J.Easton 6/3 4/6 8/6				
54. Easton, Jared (AUS)						
(WC) 55. Thompson, Michael (GBR)	C-M.Stebe [10] 6/1 6/2					
56. **Stebe, Cedrik-Marcel [10]** (GER)						
57. **Goffin, David [13]** (BEL)	A.Thomas 5/7 6/1 6/3	A.Thomas 2/6 6/4 9/7	A.Thomas 6/3 6/2			
58. Thomas, Andrew (AUS)						
59. Cox, Daniel (GBR)	D.Cox 6/2 4/6 6/2					
(LL) 60. Ndimande, Mbonisi (ZIM)						
61. Wachiramanowong, Kittipong (THA)	A.Giannessi 7/6(2) 6/4	T-H.Yang [2] 7/6(7) 6/2				
(WC) 62. Giannessi, Alessandro (ITA)						
63. Hernandez, Jose (DOM)	T-H.Yang [2] 6/4 6/3					
64. **Yang, Tsung-Hua [2]** (TPE)						

Heavy type denotes seeded players. The figure in brackets against names denotes the order in which they were seeded.
(WC)=Wild card. (Q)=Qualifier.

EVENT XI – THE BOYS' DOUBLES CHAMPIONSHIP 2008
HOLDERS: D.LOPEZ & M.TREVISAN

The Winners became the holders, for the year only, of a Cup presented by The All England Lawn Tennis and Croquet Club.
The Winners received miniature Cups and the Runners-up received mementos. The matches were best of three sets.

First Round	Second Round	Quarter-Finals	Semi-Finals	Final	Winners
1. **H.Cunha** (BRA) & **C.Ramirez** (MEX) **[1]**	A.Sanders & M.Verryth 6/3 6/4	A.Sanders & M.Verryth 6/2 7/6(5)	A.Folie & D.Goffin [5] 6/2 7/5	M.Reid & B.Tomic [3] 6/4 5/7 6/4	C-P.Hsieh & T-H.Yang 6/4 2/6 12/10
2. A.Sanders (AUS) & M.Verryth (AUS)					
(WC) 3. D.Hodgson (GBR) & A.Watling (GBR)	D.Hodgson & A.Watling 4/6 7/6(1) 6/4				
4. N.Angus (GBR) & M.Thompson (GBR)					
5. J.Hernandez (DOM) & C.Saavedra-Corvalan (CHI)	B.Puc & J-C.Spir 6/2 6/4	A.Folie & D.Goffin [5] 6/4 6/4			
6. B.Puc (SLO) & J-C.Spir (COL)					
7. T.Longhi (JPN) & K.Wachiramanowong (THA)	A.Folie & D.Goffin [5] 6/2 6/1				
8. **A.Folie** (BEL) & **D.Goffin** (BEL) **[5]**					
9. **M.Reid** (AUS) & **B.Tomic** (AUS) **[3]**	M.Reid & B.Tomic [3] 6/3 3/6 6/3	M.Reid & B.Tomic [3] 6/3 6/4	M.Reid & B.Tomic [3] 6/3 6/2		
10. N.Pauffley (GBR) & M.Willis (GBR)					
11. D.Evans (GBR) & D.Smethurst (GBR)	D.Evans & D.Smethurst 6/4 6/4				
(WC) 12. F.Akhazzan (GBR) & M.Davis (GBR)					
13. M.Draganja (CRO) & F.Krajinovic (SRB)	M.Draganja & F.Krajinovic 6/2 6/4	L.Barnes & J.Marsalek 6/4 6/4			
14. C.Boluda-Purkiss (ESP) & D.Cox (GBR)					
(WC) 15. L.Barnes (GBR) & J.Marsalek (GBR)	L.Barnes & J.Marsalek 1/6 7/6(4) 7/5				
16. **C.Buchanan** (GBR) & **J.Jenkins** (USA) **[7]**					
17. **H.Moriya** (JPN) & **P.Siributwong** (THA) **[8]**	C-P.Hsieh & T-H.Yang 7/6(4) 6/4	C-P.Hsieh & T-H.Yang 6/4 6/1	C-P.Hsieh & T-H.Yang 4/6 6/3 6/2	C-P.Hsieh & T-H.Yang 7/6(2) 2/6 7/5	
18. C-P.Hsieh (TPE) & T-H.Yang (TPE)					
19. N.Moser (AUT) & D.Propoggia (AUS)	N.Moser & D.Propoggia 7/6(6) Ret'd				
20. M.Ndimande (ZIM) & C.Rungkat (INA)					
21. E.Crepaldi (ITA) & H.Ehara (JPN)	E.Crepaldi & H.Ehara 6/3 4/6 6/2	E.Crepaldi & H.Ehara w/o			
22. D.Britton (USA) & G.Miccini (ITA)					
(A) 23. A.Bull (GBR) & K.Singh (IND)	G.Dimitrov & H.Kontinen [4] 6/1 6/2				
24. **G.Dimitrov** (BUL) & **H.Kontinen** (FIN) **[4]**					
25. **M.Arevalo** (ESA) & **T.Garanganga** (ZIM) **[6]**	V.Pospisil & M.Raonic 6/7(2) 7/5 6/4	M.Basic & D.Wu 7/5 6/7(3) 6/3	M.Basic & D.Wu 6/1 7/5		
26. V.Pospisil (CAN) & M.Raonic (CAN)					
27. M.Basic (BIH) & D.Wu (CHN)	M.Basic & D.Wu 3/6 6/1 6/4				
28. P.Lang (AUT) & C-M.Stebe (GER)					
29. Y.Bhambri (IND) & Z.Zhang (CHN)	J.Easton & A.Thomas 7/6(6) 3/6 11/9	R.Harrison & B.Klahn [2] 6/4 6/7(8) 6/3			
30. J.Easton (AUS) & A.Thomas (AUS)					
(WC) 31. M.James (GBR) & M.Short (GBR)	R.Harrison & B.Klahn [2] 7/6(4) 6/2				
32. **R.Harrison** (USA) & **B.Klahn** (USA) **[2]**					

Heavy type denotes seeded players. The figure in brackets against names denotes the order in which they were seeded.
(WC)=Wild card. (A)=Alternates

EVENT XII – THE GIRLS' SINGLES CHAMPIONSHIP 2008
HOLDER: MISS U. RADWANSKA

The Winner became the holder, for the year only, of a Cup presented by The All England Lawn Tennis and Croquet Club.
The Winner received a miniature Cup and the Runner-up received a memento. The matches were best of three sets.

First Round	Second Round	Third Round	Quarter-Finals	Semi-Finals	Final	Winner
1. **Oudin, Melanie [1]** (USA)						
(Q) 2. Ishizu, Sachie (JPN)	**Miss M.Oudin [1]** 6/1 6/2					
3. Robson, Laura (GBR)		Miss L.Robson 6/1 6/3				
(LL) 4. Guarachi, Alexa (USA)	Miss L.Robson 6/0 6/4					
5. Kerkhove, Lesley (NED)			Miss L.Robson 7/6(6) 7/5			
6. Marino, Rebecca (CAN)	Miss L.Kerkhove 3/6 6/3 6/4					
7. Jani, Reka-Luca (HUN)		Miss L.Kerkhove 5/7 6/3 6/2				
8. **Berlinecke, Linda [15]** (GER)	**Miss L.Berlinecke [15]** 6/4 6/3					
9. **Jovanovski, Bojana [9]** (SRB)	**Miss B.Jovanovski [9]** 6/0 6/1				Miss L.Robson 7/5 6/4	
10. Grymalska, Anastassia (ITA)		**Miss B.Jovanovski [9]** 6/3 6/4				
(WC) 11. Cunningham, Amanda (GBR)	Miss M.Borecka 7/5 6/2					
(Q) 12. Borecka, Martina (CZE)			Miss B.Jovanovski [9] 7/5 6/2			
13. Holland, Isabella (AUS)	Miss I.Holland 7/5 4/6 8/6					
(WC) 14. Grela, Aleksandra (POL)		Miss I.Holland 6/3 4/6 6/3				
15. Sirotkina, Marta (RUS)	Miss M.Sirotkina 7/5 3/6 6/0					
16. **Nara, Kurumi [8]** (JPN)						
17. **Bogdan, Elena [4]** (ROU)	Miss K.Mladenovic 6/2 6/1					
18. Mladenovic, Kristina (FRA)		Miss K.Mladenovic 7/6(3) 6/2				
19. Zaniewska, Sandra (POL)	Miss S.Zaniewska 6/0 6/1					
(WC) 20. Brook, Victoria (GBR)			Miss R.Tabakova 6/4 6/3			
(Q) 21. Tabakova, Romana (SVK)	Miss R.Tabakova 6/0 6/4					
(WC) 22. Rae, Jocelyn (GBR)		Miss R.Tabakova 6/1 6/1				
(Q) 23. Narattana, Kanyapat (THA)	**Miss E.Chernyakova [14]** 6/2 6/3					
24. **Chernyakova, Elena [14]** (RUS)				Miss R.Tabakova 6/4 6/1		
25. **Konta, Johanna [10]** (AUS)	**Miss J.Konta [10]** 7/5 6/1					
26. Gorny, Monica (RSA)		**Miss J.Konta [10]** 6/3 6/3				
(WC) 27. Vandeweghe, Coco (USA)	Miss J.Windley 6/2 7/5					
(Q) 28. Windley, Jade (GBR)			Miss P.Hercog [5] 3/6 6/4 6/3			
29. Lalami, Nadia (MAR)	Miss B.Gumulya 2/6 6/4 6/4					
30. Gumulya, Beatrice (INA)		**Miss P.Hercog [5]** 6/1 7/6(3)				
31. Doi, Misaki (JPN)	**Miss P.Hercog [5]** 6/4 6/2				Miss R.Tabakova 6/4 6/1	
32. **Hercog, Polona [5]** (SLO)						
33. **Bogdan, Ana [7]** (ROU)	Miss N.Broady 6/3 7/6(5)					
(WC) 34. Broady, Naomi (GBR)		Miss N.Broady 6/3 4/6 6/2				
35. Burdette, Mallory (USA)	Miss Z.Diyas 6/3 6/4					
36. Diyas, Zarina (KAZ)			Miss N.Broady 7/6(6) 6/2			
37. Buchina, Yana (RUS)	Miss M.Trevisan 6/4 4/6 6/3					
(Q) 38. Trevisan, Martina (ITA)		Miss N.Hofmanova [12] 6/2 6/2				
(Q) 39. Dabrowski, Gabriela (CAN)	**Miss N.Hofmanova [12]** 6/1 6/1					
40. **Hofmanova, Nikola [12]** (AUT)				Miss N.Broady 7/6(4) 6/3		
41. **Piter, Katarzyna [16]** (POL)	Miss K.Piter [16] 6/4 6/0					
42. Curtis, Jade (GBR)		Miss T.Calderwood 6/3 6/1				
43. Inoue, Miyabi (JPN)						
(Q) 44. Calderwood, Tyra (AUS)	Miss T.Calderwood 6/7(5) 7/6(0) 6/4					
45. Hogenkamp, Richel (NED)			Miss N.Lertcheewakarn [3] 6/2 6/2			Miss L.Robson 6/3 3/6 6/1
46. Babos, Timea (HUN)	Miss R.Hogenkamp 5/7 6/3 6/3					
47. Linhova, Zuzana (CZE)		**Miss N.Lertcheewakarn [3]** 6/3 6/1				
48. **Lertcheewakarn, Noppawan [3]** (THA)	**Miss N.Lertcheewakarn [3]** 4/6 6/0 6/1				Miss N.Lertcheewakarn [3] 6/7(6) 6/3 6/4	
49. **Moore, Jessica [6]** (AUS)	**Miss J.Moore [6]** 4/6 6/3 6/1					
50. Venkatesh, Poojashree (IND)		**Miss J.Moore [6]** 6/3 6/4				
51. Luknarova, Zuzana (SVK)	Miss Z.Luknarova 6/3 3/6 6/4					
(WC) 52. Watson, Heather (GBR)			Miss T.Hendler 6/3 6/3			
53. Hendler, Tamaryn (BEL)	Miss T.Hendler 6/3 4/6 6/1					
54. Chala, Cindy (FRA)		Miss T.Hendler 6/0 6/4				
55. Burnett, Nastassya (ITA)	Miss N.Burnett 7/6(5) 6/3					
56. **Lykina, Ksenia [11]** (RUS)				Miss T.Hendler 7/6(4) 6/3		
57. **Rompies, Jessy [13]** (INA)	Miss A.Yamasoto 6/7(3) 6/1 6/2					
58. Yamasoto, Aki (JPN)		Miss Z.Susanyi 6/4 7/6(4)				Miss N.Lertcheewakarn [3] 7/6(2) 6/3
59. Susanyi, Zsofia (HUN)	Miss Z.Susanyi 7/6(5) 6/4					
(WC) 60. Moore, Tara (GBR)			Miss A.Rus [2] 6/0 6/4			
61. Yang, Zi-Jun (HKG)	Miss Z-J.Yang 6/2 6/1					
62. Orlik, Anna (BLR)		**Miss A.Rus [2]** 6/3 6/0				
63. Spremo, Milana (SRB)						
64. **Rus, Arantxa [2]** (NED)	**Miss A.Rus [2]** 6/1 6/3					

Heavy type denotes seeded players. The figure in brackets against names denotes the order in which they were seeded.
(WC)=Wild card. (Q)=Qualifier. (LL)=Lucky Loser.

EVENT XIII – THE GIRLS' DOUBLES CHAMPIONSHIP 2008
HOLDERS: MISS A. PAVLYUCHENKOVA & MISS U. RADWANSKA

The Winners became the holders, for the year only, of a Cup presented by The All England Lawn Tennis and Croquet Club.
The Winners received miniature Cups and the Runners-up received mementoes. The matches were best of three sets.

First Round	Second Round	Quarter-Finals	Semi-Finals	Final	Winners
1. **Miss E.Bogdan** (ROU) & **Miss B.Jovanovski** (SRB) **[1]**					
2. Miss M.Ejdesgaard (DEN) & Miss G.Piven (UKR)	**Miss E.Bogdan & Miss B.Jovanovski [1]** 6/1 7/5				
3. Miss T.Calderwood (AUS) & Miss J.Konta (AUS)		**Miss E.Bogdan & Miss B.Jovanovski [1]** 6/7(6) 7/6(4) 7/5			
4. Miss M.Inoue (JPN) & Miss A.Yamasoto (JPN)	Miss T.Calderwood & Miss J.Konta 6/3 6/4				
5. Miss R.Hogenkamp (NED) & Miss L.Robson (GBR)			Miss P.Hercog & Miss J.Moore [6] 6/1 6/3		
6. Miss Z.Linhova (CZE) & Miss Z.Luknarova (SVK)	Miss Z.Linhova & Miss Z.Luknarova 4/6 7/6(3) 6/2				
7. Miss K.Narattana (THA) & Miss Z-J.Yang (HKG)		**Miss P.Hercog & Miss J.Moore [6]** 6/3 6/0			
8. **Miss P.Hercog** (SLO) & **Miss J.Moore** (AUS) **[6]**	**Miss P.Hercog & Miss J.Moore [6]** 6/3 6/3				
9. **Miss E.Chernyakova** (RUS) & **Miss N.Hofmanova** (AUT) **[4]**	**Miss E.Chernyakova & Miss N.Hofmanova [4]** 6/3 4/6 6/3				
10. Miss A.Orlik (BLR) & Miss M.Sirotkina (RUS)		Miss J.Curtis & Miss J.Rae 6/3 6/3			
11. Miss G.Dabrowski (CAN) & Miss S.Ishizu (JPN)	Miss J.Curtis & Miss J.Rae 7/6(2) 6/1				
(WC) 12. Miss J.Curtis (GBR) & Miss J.Rae (GBR)			Miss J.Curtis & Miss J.Rae 6/4 7/6(2)		
(WC) 13. Miss A.Cunningham (GBR) & Miss L.Slater (GBR)	Miss A.Grymalska & Miss N.Lalami 6/3 6/2				
14. Miss A.Grymalska (ITA) & Miss N.Lalami (MAR)		**Miss L.Kerkhove & Miss A.Rus [5]** 6/2 6/2			
15. Miss Y.Buchina (RUS) & Miss Z.Diyas (KAZ)					
16. **Miss L.Kerkhove** (NED) & **Miss A.Rus** (NED) **[5]**	**Miss L.Kerkhove & Miss A.Rus [5]** 7/6(4) 6/2			Miss P.Hercog & Miss J.Moore [6] 4/6 6/3 6/4	
17. **Miss T.Babos** (HUN) & **Miss R-L.Jani** (HUN) **[8]**					
(A) 18. Miss T.Hendler (BEL) & Miss C.Vandeweghe (USA)	**Miss T.Babos & Miss R-L.Jani [8]** wo.				
19. Miss A.Grela (POL) & Miss S.Zaniewska (POL)		**Miss T.Babos & Miss R-L.Jani [8]** 7/5 6/2			
(WC) 20. Miss N.Broady (GBR) & Miss J.Windley (GBR)	Miss N.Broady & Miss J.Windley 6/7(4) 6/2 6/4				
(A) 21. Miss V.Brook (GBR) & Miss S.Cornish (GBR)			Miss M.Doi & Miss K.Nara 7/5 6/7(7) 6/1		
22. Miss M.Gorny (RSA) & Miss R.Marino (CAN)	Miss M.Gorny & Miss R.Marino 6/2 7/5				
23. Miss M.Doi (JPN) & Miss K.Nara (JPN)		**Miss M.Doi & Miss K.Nara** 6/3 5/7 9/7			
24. **Miss M.Burdette** (USA) & **Miss M.Oudin** (USA) **[3]**	Miss M.Doi & Miss K.Nara 6/3 5/7 9/7			Miss M.Doi & Miss K.Nara 1/6 6/2 6/1	Miss P.Hercog & Miss J.Moore [6] 6/3 1/6 6/2
25. **Miss C.Chala** (FRA) & **Miss N.Lertcheewakarn** (THA) **[7]**					
26. Miss K.Piter (POL) & Miss R.Tabakova (SVK)	Miss K.Piter & Miss R.Tabakova 7/5 6/1				
(WC) 27. Miss T.Moore (GBR) & Miss H.Watson (GBR)		Miss T.Moore & Miss H.Watson 6/3 5/7 9/7			
28. Miss B.Otashliyska (BUL) & Miss A.Sotnikova (UKR)	Miss T.Moore & Miss H.Watson 6/3 6/3				
29. Miss B.Gumulya (INA) & Miss J.Rompies (INA)			Miss I.Holland & Miss S.Peers 6/3 3/6 9/7		
30. Miss I.Holland (AUS) & Miss S.Peers (AUS)	Miss I.Holland & Miss S.Peers 6/7(5) 6/2 6/4				
31. Miss M.Spremo (SRB) & Miss Z.Susanyi (HUN)		**Miss I.Holland & Miss S.Peers** 6/2 7/5			
32. **Miss A.Bogdan** (ROU) & **Miss K.Lykina** (RUS) **[2]**	**Miss A.Bogdan & Miss K.Lykina [2]** 6/1 6/2				

Heavy type denotes seeded players. The figure in brackets against names denotes the order in which they were seeded.
(A)=Alternates. (WC)=Wild card.

THE CHAMPIONSHIP ROLL
GENTLEMEN'S SINGLES — CHAMPIONS & RUNNERS UP

1877 S. W. Gore
W. C. Marshall

1878 P. F. Hadow
S. W. Gore

* 1879 J. T. Hartley
V. St. L. Goold

1880 J. T. Hartley
H. F. Lawford

1881 W. Renshaw
J. T. Hartley

1882 W. Renshaw
E. Renshaw

1883 W. Renshaw
E. Renshaw

1884 W. Renshaw
H. F. Lawford

1885 W. Renshaw
H. F. Lawford

1886 W. Renshaw
H. F. Lawford

* 1887 H. F. Lawford
E. Renshaw

1888 E. Renshaw
H. F. Lawford

1889 W. Renshaw
E. Renshaw

1890 W. J. Hamilton
W. Renshaw

* 1891 W. Baddeley
J. Pim

1892 W. Baddeley
J. Pim

1893 J. Pim
W. Baddeley

1894 J. Pim
W. Baddeley

* 1895 W. Baddeley
W. V. Eaves

1896 H. S. Mahony
W. Baddeley

1897 R. F. Doherty
H. S. Mahony

1898 R. F. Doherty
H. L . Doherty

1899 R. F. Doherty
A. W. Gore

1900 R. F. Doherty
S. H. Smith

1901 A. W. Gore
R. F. Doherty

1902 H. L. Doherty
A. W. Gore

1903 H. L. Doherty
F. L. Riseley

1904 H. L. Doherty
F. L. Riseley

1905 H. L. Doherty
N. E. Brookes

1906 H. L. Doherty
F. L. Riseley

* 1907 N. E. Brookes
A. W. Gore

* 1908 A. W. Gore
H. Roper Barrett

1909 A. W. Gore
M. J. G. Ritchie

1910 A. F. Wilding
A. W. Gore

1911 A. F. Wilding
H. Roper Barrett

1912 A. F. Wilding
A. W. Gore

1913 A. F. Wilding
M. E. McLoughlin

1914 N. E. Brookes
A. F. Wilding

1919 G. L. Patterson
N. E. Brookes

1920 W. T. Tilden
G. L. Patterson

1921 W. T. Tilden
B. I. C. Norton

*† 1922 G. L. Patterson
R. Lycett

* 1923 W. M. Johnston
F. T. Hunter

* 1924 J. Borotra
R. Lacoste

1925 R. Lacoste
J. Borotra

* 1926 J. Borotra
H. Kinsey

1927 H. Cochet
J. Borotra

1928 R. Lacoste
H. Cochet

* 1929 H. Cochet
J. Borotra

1930 W. T. Tilden
W. Allison

* 1931 S. B. Wood
F. X. Shields

1932 H. E. Vines
H. W. Austin

1933 J. H. Crawford
H. E. Vines

1934 F. J. Perry
J. H. Crawford

1935 F. J. Perry
G. von Cramm

1936 F. J. Perry
G. von Cramm

* 1937 J. D. Budge
G. von Cramm

1938 J. D. Budge
H. W. Austin

* 1939 R. L. Riggs
E. T. Cooke

* 1946 Y. Petra
G. E. Brown

1947 J. Kramer
T. Brown

* 1948 R. Falkenburg
J. E. Bromwich

1949 F. R. Schroeder
J. Drobny

* 1950 B. Patty
F. A. Sedgman

1951 R. Savitt
K. McGregor

1952 F. A. Sedgman
J. Drobny

* 1953 V. Seixas
K. Nielsen

1954 J. Drobny
K. R. Rosewall

1955 T. Trabert
K. Nielsen

* 1956 L. A. Hoad
K. R. Rosewall

1957 L. A. Hoad
A. J. Cooper

* 1958 A. J. Cooper
N. A. Fraser

* 1959 A. Olmedo
R. Laver

* 1960 N. A. Fraser
R. Laver

1961 R. Laver
C. R. McKinley

1962 R. Laver
M. F. Mulligan

* 1963 C. R. McKinley
F. S. Stolle

1964 R. Emerson
F. S. Stolle

1965 R. Emerson
F. S. Stolle

1966 M. Santana
R. D. Ralston

1967 J. D. Newcombe
W. P. Bungert

1968 R. Laver
A. D. Roche

1969 R. Laver
J. D. Newcombe

1970 J. D. Newcombe
K. R. Rosewall

1971 J. D. Newcombe
S. R. Smith

* 1972 S. R. Smith
I. Nastase

* 1973 J. Kodes
A. Metreveli

1974 J. S. Connors
K. R. Rosewall

1975 A. R. Ashe
J. S. Connors

1976 B. Borg
I. Nastase

1977 B. Borg
J. S. Connors

1978 B. Borg
J. S.Connors

1979 B. Borg
R. Tanner

1980 B. Borg
J. P. McEnroe

1981 J. P. McEnroe
B. Borg

1982 J. S. Connors
J. P. McEnroe

1983 J. P. McEnroe
C. J. Lewis

1984 J. P. McEnroe
J. S. Connors

1985 B. Becker
K. Curren

1986 B.Becker
I. Lendl

1987 P. Cash
I. Lendl

1988 S. Edberg
B. Becker

1989 B. Becker
S. Edberg

1990 S. Edberg
B. Becker

1991 M. Stich
B. Becker

1992 A. Agassi
G. Ivanisevic

1993 P. Sampras
J. Courier

1994 P. Sampras
G. Ivanisevic

1995 P. Sampras
B. Becker

1996 R. Krajicek
M. Washington

1997 P. Sampras
C. Pioline

1998 P. Sampras
G. Ivanisevic

1999 P. Sampras
A. Agassi

2000 P. Sampras
P. Rafter

2001 G. Ivanisevic
P. Rafter

2002 L. Hewitt
D. Nalbandian

2003 R. Federer
M. Philippoussis

2004 R. Federer
A. Roddick

2005 R. Federer
A. Roddick

2006 R. Federer
R. Nadal

2007 R. Federer
R. Nadal

2008 R. Nadal
R. Federer

*For the years 1913, 1914 and 1919-1923 inclusive the above records include the "World's Championships on Grass" granted to The Lawn Tennis Association by The International Lawn Tennis Federation. This title was then abolished and commencing in 1924 they became The OYcial Lawn Tennis Championships recognised by The International Lawn Tennis Federation. Prior to 1922 the holders in the Singles Events and Gentlemen's Doubles did not compete in the Championships but met the winners of these events in the Challenge Rounds. † Challenge Round abolished: holders subsequently played through. * The holder did not defend the title.*

THE CHAMPIONSHIP ROLL
LADIES' SINGLES—CHAMPIONS & RUNNERS UP

1884 Miss M. Watson *Miss L. Watson*	1907 Miss M. Sutton *Mrs. Lambert Chambers*	* 1934 Miss D. E. Round *Miss H. H. Jacobs*	* 1963 Miss M. Smith *Miss B. J. Moffitt*	1986 Miss M. Navratilova *Miss H. Mandlikova*
1885 Miss M. Watson *Miss B. Bingley*	* 1908 Mrs. A. Sterry *Miss A. M. Morton*	1935 Mrs. F. S. Moody *Miss H. H. Jacobs*	1964 Miss M. E. Bueno *Miss M. Smith*	1987 Miss M. Navratilova *Miss S. Graf*
1886 Miss B. Bingley *Miss M. Watson*	* 1909 Miss D. P. Boothby *Miss A. M. Morton*	* 1936 Miss H. H. Jacobs *Frau. S. Sperling*	1965 Miss M. Smith *Miss M. E. Bueno*	1988 Miss S. Graf *Miss M. Navratilova*
1887 Miss L. Dod *Miss B. Bingley*	1910 Mrs. Lambert Chambers *Miss D. P. Boothby*	1937 Miss D. E. Round *Miss J. Jedrzejowska*	1966 Mrs. L. W. King *Miss M. E. Bueno*	1989 Miss S. Graf *Miss M. Navratilova*
1888 Miss L. Dod *Mrs. G. W. Hillyard*	1911 Mrs. Lambert Chambers *Miss D. P. Boothby*	* 1938 Mrs. F. S. Moody *Miss H. H. Jacobs*	1967 Mrs. L. W. King *Mrs. P. F. Jones*	1990 Miss M. Navratilova *Miss Z. Garrison*
* 1889 Mrs. G. W. Hillyard *Miss L. Rice*	* 1912 Mrs. D. R. Larcombe *Mrs. A. Sterry*	* 1939 Miss A. Marble *Miss K. E. Stammers*	1968 Mrs. L. W. King *Miss J. A. M. Tegart*	1991 Miss S. Graf *Miss G. Sabatini*
* 1890 Miss L. Rice *Miss M. Jacks*	* 1913 Mrs. Lambert Chambers *Mrs. R. J. McNair*	* 1946 Miss P. Betz *Miss L. Brough*	1969 Mrs. P. F. Jones *Mrs. L. W. King*	1992 Miss S. Graf *Miss M. Seles*
* 1891 Miss L. Dod *Mrs. G. W. Hillyard*	1914 Mrs. Lambert Chambers *Mrs. D. R. Larcombe*	* 1947 Miss M. Osborne *Miss D. Hart*	* 1970 Mrs. B. M. Court *Mrs. L. W. King*	1993 Miss S. Graf *Miss J. Novotna*
1892 Miss L. Dod *Mrs. G. W. Hillyard*	1919 Mlle. S. Lenglen *Mrs. Lambert Chambers*	1948 Miss L. Brough *Miss D. Hart*	1971 Miss E. F. Goolagong *Mrs. B. M. Court*	1994 Miss C. Martinez *Miss M. Navratilova*
1893 Miss L. Dod *Mrs. G. W. Hillyard*	1920 Mlle. S. Lenglen *Mrs. Lambert Chambers*	1949 Miss L. Brough *Mrs. W. du Pont*	1972 Mrs. L. W. King *Miss E. F. Goolagong*	1995 Miss S. Graf *Miss A. Sanchez Vicario*
* 1894 Mrs. G. W. Hillyard *Miss E. L. Austin*	1921 Mlle. S. Lenglen *Miss E. Ryan*	1950 Miss L. Brough *Mrs. W. du Pont*	1973 Mrs. L. W. King *Miss C. M. Evert*	1996 Miss S. Graf *Miss A. Sanchez Vicario*
* 1895 Miss C. Cooper *Miss H. Jackson*	† 1922 Mlle. S. Lenglen *Mrs. F. Mallory*	1951 Miss D. Hart *Miss S. Fry*	1974 Miss C. M. Evert *Mrs. O. Morozova*	* 1997 Miss M. Hingis *Miss J. Novotna*
1896 Miss C. Cooper *Mrs. W. H.Pickering*	1923 Mlle. S. Lenglen *Miss K. McKane*	1952 Miss M. Connolly *Miss L. Brough*	1975 Mrs. L. W. King *Mrs. R. Cawley*	1998 Miss J. Novotna *Miss N. Tauziat*
1897 Mrs. G. W. Hillyard *Miss C. Cooper*	1924 Miss K. McKane *Miss H. Wills*	1953 Miss M. Connolly *Miss D. Hart*	* 1976 Miss C. M. Evert *Mrs. R. Cawley*	1999 Miss L.A. Davenport *Miss S. Graf*
* 1898 Miss C. Cooper *Miss L Martin*	1925 Mlle. S. Lenglen *Miss J. Fry*	1954 Miss M. Connolly *Miss L. Brough*	1977 Miss S. V. Wade *Miss B. F. Stove*	2000 Miss V. Williams *Miss L.A. Davenport*
1899 Mrs. G. W. Hillyard *Miss C. Cooper*	1926 Mrs. L. A. Godfree *Sta. L. de Alvarez*	* 1955 Miss L. Brough *Mrs. J. G. Fleitz*	1978 Miss M. Navratilova *Miss C. M. Evert*	2001 Miss V. Williams *Miss J. Henin*
1900 Mrs. G. W. Hillyard *Miss C. Cooper*	1927 Miss H. Wills *Sta. L. de Alvarez*	1956 Miss S. Fry *Miss A. Buxton*	1979 Miss M. Navratilova *Mrs. J. M. Lloyd*	2002 Miss S. Williams *Miss V. Williams*
1901 Mrs. A. Sterry *Mrs. G. W. Hillyard*	1928 Miss H. Wills *Sta. L. de Alvarez*	* 1957 Miss A. Gibson *Miss D. R. Hard*	1980 Mrs. R. Cawley *Mrs. J. M. Lloyd*	2003 Miss S. Williams *Miss V. Williams*
1902 Miss M. E. Robb *Mrs. A. Sterry*	1929 Miss H. Wills *Miss H. H. Jacobs*	1958 Miss A. Gibson *Miss A. Mortimer*	* 1981 Mrs. J. M. Lloyd *Miss H. Mandlikova*	2004 Miss M. Sharapova *Miss S. Williams*
* 1903 Miss D. K. Douglass *Miss E. W. Thomson*	1930 Mrs. F. S. Moody *Miss E. Ryan*	* 1959 Miss M. E. Bueno *Miss D. R. Hard*	1982 Miss M. Navratilova *Mrs. J. M. Lloyd*	2005 Miss V. Williams *Miss L. Davenport*
1904 Miss D. K. Douglass *Mrs. A. Sterry*	* 1931 Fraulein C. Aussem *Fraulein H. Krahwinkel*	1960 Miss M. E. Bueno *Miss S. Reynolds*	1983 Miss M. Navratilova *Miss A. Jaeger*	2006 Miss A. Mauresmo *Mrs J. Henin-Hardenne*
1905 Miss M. Sutton *Miss D. K. Douglass*	* 1932 Mrs. F. S. Moody *Miss H. H. Jacobs*	* 1961 Miss A. Mortimer *Miss C. C. Truman*	1984 Miss M. Navratilova *Mrs. J. M. Lloyd*	2007 Miss V. Williams *Miss M. Bartoli*
1906 Miss D. K. Douglass *Miss M. Sutton*	1933 Mrs. F. S. Moody *Miss D. E. Round*	1962 Mrs. J. R. Susman *Mrs. V. Sukova*	1985 Miss M. Navratilova *Mrs. J. M. Lloyd*	2008 Miss V. Williams *Miss S. Williams*

MAIDEN NAMES OF LADY CHAMPIONS (*In the tables the following have been recorded in both married and single identities*)

MRS. R. CAWLEY ....MISS E. F. GOOLAGONG	MRS J. HENIN-HARDENNE ....MISS J. HENIN	MRS. O. MOROZOVA ....MISS O. MOROZOVA
MRS. LAMBERT CHAMBERS................MISS D. K. DOUGLASS	MRS. G. W. HILLYARD.....................MISS B. BINGLEY	MRS. L. E. G. PRICE ....MISS S. REYNOLDS
MRS. B. M. COURT ....MISS M. SMITH	MRS. P. F. JONES ....MISS A. S. HAYDON	MRS. G. E. REID ....MISS K. MELVILLE
MRS. B. C. COVELL ....MISS P. L. HOWKINS	MRS. L. W. KING ....MISS B. J. MOFFITT	MRS. P. D. SMYLIE ....MISS E. M. SAYERS
MRS. D. E. DALTON..........................MISS J. A. M. TEGART	MRS. M. R. KING..............................MISS P. E. MUDFORD	FRAU. S. SPERLING.........................FRAULEIN H. KRAHWINKEL
MRS. W. DU PONT ....MISS M. OSBORNE	MRS. D. R. LARCOMBE ....MISS E. W. THOMSON	MRS. A. STERRY ....MISS C. COOPER
MRS. L. A. GODFREE........................MISS K. MCKANE	MRS. J. M. LLOYD ....MISS C. M. EVERT	MRS. J. R. SUSMAN ....MISS K. HANTZE
MRS. H. F. GOURLAY CAWLEY ....MISS H. F. GOURLAY	MRS. F. S. MOODY ....MISS H. WILLS	

THE CHAMPIONSHIP ROLL

GENTLEMEN'S DOUBLES—CHAMPIONS & RUNNERS UP

Year	Champions	Runners up
1879	L. R. Erskine & H. F. Lawford	*F. Durant & G. E. Tabor*
1880	W. Renshaw & E. Renshaw	*O. E. Woodhouse & C. J. Cole*
1881	W. Renshaw & E. Renshaw	*W. J. Down & H. Vaughan*
1882	J. T. Hartley & R. T. Richardson	*J. G. Horn & C. B. Russell*
1883	C. W. Grinstead & C. E. Welldon	*C. B. Russell & R. T. Milford*
1884	W. Renshaw & E. Renshaw	*E. W. Lewis & E. L Williams*
1885	W. Renshaw & E. Renshaw	*C. E. Farrer & A. J. Stanley*
1886	W. Renshaw & E. Renshaw	*C. E. Farrer & A. J. Stanley*
1887	P. Bowes-Lyon & H. W. W. Wilberforce	*J. H. Crispe & E. Barratt Smith*
1888	W. Renshaw & E. Renshaw	*P Bowes-Lyon & H. W. W. Wilberforce*
1889	W. Renshaw & E. Renshaw	*E. W. Lewis & G. W. Hillyard*
1890	J. Pim & F. O. Stoker	*E. W. Lewis & G. W. Hillyard*
1891	W. Baddeley & H. Baddeley	*J. Pim & F. O. Stoker*
1892	H. S. Barlow & E. W. Lewis	*W. Baddeley & H. Baddeley*
1893	J. Pim & F. O. Stoker	*E. W. Lewis & H. S. Barlow*
1894	W. Baddeley & H. Baddeley	*H. S. Barlow & C. H. Martin*
1895	W. Baddeley & H. Baddeley	*E. W. Lewis & W. V. Eaves*
1896	W. Baddeley & H. Baddeley	*R. F. Doherty & H. A. Nisbet*
1897	R. F. Doherty & H. L. Doherty	*W. Baddeley & H. Baddeley*
1898	R. F. Doherty & H. L . Doherty	*H. A. Nisbet & C. Hobart*
1899	R. F. Doherty & H. L. Doherty	*H. A. Nisbet & C. Hobart*
1900	R. F. Doherty & H. L. Doherty	*H. Roper Barrett & H. A. Nisbet*
1901	R. F. Doherty & H. L. Doherty	*Dwight Davis & Holcombe Ward*
1902	S. H. Smith & F. L. Riseley	*R. F. Doherty & H. L. Doherty*
1903	R. F. Doherty & H. L. Doherty	*S. H. Smith & F. L. Riseley*
1904	R. F. Doherty & H. L. Doherty	*S. H. Smith & F. L. Riseley*
1905	R. F. Doherty & H. L. Doherty	*S. H. Smith & F. L. Riseley*
1906	S. H. Smith & F. L. Riseley	*R. F. Doherty & H. L. Doherty*
1907	N. E. Brookes & A. F. Wilding	*B. C. Wright & K. H. Behr*
1908	A. F. Wilding & M. J. G. Ritchie	*A. W. Gore & H. Roper Barrett*
1909	A. W. Gore & H. Roper Barrett	*S. N. Doust & H. A. Parker*
1910	A. F. Wilding & M. J. G. Ritchie	*A. W. Gore & H. Roper Barrett*
1911	M. Decugis & A. H. Gobert	*M. J. G. Ritchie & A. F. Wilding*
1912	H. Roper Barrett & C. P. Dixon	*M. Decugis & A. H. Gobert*
1913	H. Roper Barrett & C. P. Dixon	*F. W. Rahe & H. Kleinschroth*
1914	N. E. Brookes & A. F. Wilding	*H. Roper Barrett & C. P. Dixon*
1919	R. V. Thomas & P. O'Hara-Wood	*R. Lycett & R. W. Heath*
1920	R. N. Williams & C. S. Garland	*A. R. F. Kingscote & J. C. Parke*
1921	R. Lycett & M. Woosnam	*F. G. Lowe & A. H. Lowe*
1922	R. Lycett & J. O. Anderson	*G. L. Patterson & P. O'Hara-Wood*
1923	R. Lycett & L. A. Godfree	*Count de Gomar & E. Flaquer*
1924	F. T. Hunter & V. Richards	*R. N. Williams & W. M. Washburn*
1925	J. Borotra & R. Lacoste	*J. Hennessey & R. Casey*
1926	H. Cochet & J. Brugnon	*V. Richards & H. Kinsey*
1927	F. T. Hunter & W. T. Tilden	*J. Brugnon & H. Cochet*
1928	H. Cochet & J. Brugnon	*G. L. Patterson & J. B. Hawkes*
1929	W. Allison & J. Van Ryn	*J. C. Gregory & I. G. Collins*
1930	W. Allison & J. Van Ryn	*J. H. Doeg & G. M. Lott*
1931	G. M Lott & J. Van Ryn	*H. Cochet & J. Brugnon*
1932	J. Borotra & J. Brugnon	*G. P. Hughes & F. J. Perry*
1933	J. Borotra & J. Brugnon	*R. Nunoi & J. Satoh*
1934	G. M. Lott & L. R. Stoefen	*J. Borotra & J. Brugnon*
1935	J. H. Crawford & A. K. Quist	*W. Allison & J. Van Ryn*
1936	G. P. Hughes & C. R. D. Tuckey	*C. E. Hare & F. H. D. Wilde*
1937	J. D. Budge & G. Mako	*G. P. Hughes & C. R. D. Tuckey*
1938	J. D. Budge & G. Mako	*H. Henkel & G. von Metaxa*
1939	R. L. Riggs & E. T. Cooke	*C. E. Hare & F. H. D. Wilde*
1946	T. Brown & J. Kramer	*G. E. Brown & D. Pails*
1947	R. Falkenburg & J. Kramer	*A. J. Mottram & O. W. Sidwell*
1948	J. E. Bromwich & F. A. Sedgman	*T. Brown & G. Mulloy*
1949	R. Gonzales & F. Parker	*G. Mulloy & F. R. Schroeder*
1950	J. E. Bromwich & A. K. Quist	*G. E. Brown & O. W Sidwell*
1951	K. McGregor & F. A. Sedgman	*J. Drobny & E. W. Sturgess*
1952	K. McGregor & F. A. Sedgman	*V. Seixas & E. W. Sturgess*
1953	L. A. Hoad & K. R. Rosewall	*R. N. Hartwig & M. G. Rose*
1954	R. N. Hartwig & M. G. Rose	*V. Seixas & T. Trabert*
1955	R. N. Hartwig & L. A. Hoad	*N. A. Fraser & K. R. Rosewall*
1956	L. A. Hoad & K. R. Rosewall	*N. Pietrangeli & O. Sirola*
1957	G. Mulloy & B. Patty	*N. A. Fraser & L. A. Hoad*
1958	S. Davidson & U. Schmidt	*A. J. Cooper & N. A. Fraser*
1959	R. Emerson & N. A. Fraser	*R. Laver & R. Mark*
1960	R. H. Osuna & R. D. Ralston	*M. G. Davies & R. K. Wilson*
1961	R. Emerson & N. A. Fraser	*R. A. J. Hewitt & F. S. Stolle*
1962	R. A. J. Hewitt & F. S. Stolle	*B. Jovanovic & N. Pilic*
1963	R. H. Osuna & A. Palafox	*J. C. Barclay & P. Darmon*
1964	R. A. J. Hewitt & F. S. Stolle	*R. Emerson & K. N. Fletcher*
1965	J. D. Newcombe & A. D. Roche	*K. N. Fletcher & R. A. J. Hewitt*
1966	K. N. Fletcher & J. D. Newcombe	*W. W. Bowrey & O. K. Davidson*
1967	R. A. J. Hewitt & F. D. McMillan	*R. Emerson & K. N. Fletcher*
1968	J. D. Newcombe & A. D. Roche	*K. R. Rosewall & F. S. Stolle*
1969	J. D. Newcombe & A. D. Roche	*T. S. Okker & M. C. Reissen*
1970	J. D. Newcombe & A. D. Roche	*K. R. Rosewall & F. S. Stolle*
1971	R. S. Emerson & R. G. Laver	*A. R. Ashe & R. D. Ralston*
1972	R. A. J. Hewitt & F. D. McMillan	*S. R. Smith & E. J. van Dillen*
1973	J. S. Connors & I. Nastase	*J. R. Cooper & N. A. Fraser*
1974	J. D. Newcombe & A. D. Roche	*R. C. Lutz & S. R. Smith*
1975	V. Gerulaitis & A. Mayer	*C. Dowdeswell & A. J. Stone*
1976	B. E. Gottfried & R. Ramirez	*R. L. Case & G. Masters*
1977	R. L. Case & G. Masters	*J. G. Alexander & P. C. Dent*
1978	R. A. J. Hewitt & F. D. McMillan	*P. Fleming & J. P. McEnroe*
1979	P. Fleming & J. P . McEnroe	*B. E. Gottfried & R. Ramirez*
1980	P. McNamara & P. McNamee	*R. C. Lutz & S. R. Smith*
1981	P. Fleming & J. P. McEnroe	*R. C. Lutz & S. R. Smith*
1982	P. McNamara & P. McNamee	*P. Fleming & J. P. McEnroe*
1983	P. Fleming & J. P McEnroe	*T. E. Gullikson & T. R. Gullikson*
1984	P. Fleming & J. P. McEnroe	*P. Cash & P. McNamee*
1985	H. P. Guenthardt & B. Taroczy	*P. Cash & J. B. Fitzgerald*
1986	J. Nystrom & M. Wilander	*G. Donnelly & P. Fleming*
1987	K. Flach & R. Seguso	*S. Casal & E. Sanchez*
1988	K. Flach & R. Seguso	*J. B. Fitzgerald & A. Jarryd*
1989	J. B. Fitzgerald & A. Jarryd	*R. Leach & J. Pugh*
1990	R. Leach & J. Pugh	*P. Aldrich & D. T. Visser*
1991	J. B. Fitzgerald & A. Jarryd	*J. Frana & L. Lavalle*
1992	J. P. McEnroe & M. Stich	*J. Grabb & R. A. Reneberg*
1993	T. A. Woodbridge & M. Woodforde	*G. Connell & P. Galbraith*
1994	T. A. Woodbridge & M. Woodforde	*G. Connell & P. Galbraith*
1995	T. A. Woodbridge & M. Woodforde	*R. Leach & S. Melville*
1996	T. A. Woodbridge & M. Woodforde	*B. Black & G. Connell*
1997	T. A. Woodbridge & M. Woodforde	*J. Eltingh & P. Haarhuis*
1998	J. Eltingh & P. Haarhuis	*T. A. Woodbridge & M. Woodforde*
1999	M. Bhupathi & L. Paes	*P. Haarhuis & J. Palmer*
2000	T. A. Woodbridge & M. Woodforde	*P. Haarhuis & S. Stolle*
2001	D. Johnson & J. Palmer	*J. Novak & D. Rikl*
2002	J. Bjorkman & T. A Woodbridge	*M. Knowles & D. Nestor*
2003	J. Bjorkman & T. A Woodbridge	*M. Bhupathi & M. Mirnyi*
2004	J. Bjorkman & T. A Woodbridge	*J. Knowle & N. Zimonjic*
2005	S. Huss & W. Moodie	*B. Bryan & M. Bryan*
2006	B. Bryan & M. Bryan	*F. Santoro & N. Zimonjic*
2007	A. Clement & M. Llodra	*B. Bryan & M. Bryan*
2008	D. Nestor & N. Zimonjic	*J. Bjorkman & K. Ullyett*

LADIES' DOUBLES—CHAMPIONS & RUNNERS UP

Year	Champions	Runners up
1913	Mrs. R. J. McNair & Miss D. P. Boothby	*Mrs. A. Sterry & Mrs. Lambert Chambers*
1914	Miss E. Ryan & Miss A. M. Morton	*Mrs. D. R. Larcombe & Mrs. F. J. Hannam*
1919	Mlle. S. Lenglen & Miss E. Ryan	*Mrs. Lambert Chambers & Mrs. D. R. Larcombe*
1920	Mlle. S. Lenglen & Miss E. Ryan	*Mrs. Lambert Chambers & Mrs. D. R. Larcombe*
1921	Mlle. S. Lenglen & Miss E. Ryan	*Mrs. A. E. Beamish & Mrs. G. E. Peacock*
1922	Mlle. S. Lenglen & Miss E. Ryan	*Mrs. A. D. Stocks & Miss K. McKane*
1923	Mlle. S. Lenglen & Miss E. Ryan	*Miss J. Austin & Miss E. L. Colyer*
1924	Mrs. H. Wightman & Miss H. Wills	*Mrs. B. C. Covell & Miss K. McKane*
1925	Mlle. S. Lenglen & Miss E. Ryan	*Mrs. A. V. Bridge & Mrs. C. G. McIlquham*
1926	Miss E. Ryan & Miss M. K. Browne	*Mrs. L. A. Godfree & Miss E. L. Colyer*
1927	Miss H. Wills & Miss E. Ryan	*Miss E. L. Heine & Mrs. G. E. Peacock*
1928	Mrs. Holcroft-Watson & Miss P. Saunders	*Miss E. H. Harvey & Miss E. Bennett*
1929	Mrs. Holcroft-Watson & Mrs. L.R.C. Michell	*Mrs. B. C. Covell & Mrs. D. C. Shepherd-Barron*
1930	Mrs. F. S. Moody & Miss E. Ryan	*Miss E. Cross & Miss S. Palfrey*
1931	Mrs.D.C. Shepherd-Barron & MissP.E. Mudford	*Mlle. D. Metaxa & Mlle. J. Sigart*
1932	Mlle. D. Metaxa & Mlle. J. Sigart	*Miss E. Ryan & Miss H. H. Jacobs*
1933	Mme. R. Mathieu & Miss E. Ryan	*Miss F. James & Miss A. M. Yorke*
1934	Mme. R. Mathieu & Miss E. Ryan	*Mrs. D. Andrus & Mme. S. Henrotin*
1935	Miss F. James & Miss K. E. Stammers	*Mme. R. Mathieu & Frau. S. Sperling*
1936	Miss F. James & Miss K. E. Stammers	*Mrs. S. P. Fabyan & Miss H. H. Jacobs*
1937	Mme. R. Mathieu & Miss A. M. Yorke	*Mrs. M. R. King & Mrs. J. B. Pittman*
1938	Mrs. S. P. Fabyan & Miss A. Marble	*Mme. R. Mathieu & Miss A. M. Yorke*
1939	Mrs S. P. Fabyan & Miss A. Marble	*Miss H. H. Jacobs & Miss A. M. Yorke*
1946	Miss L. Brough & Miss M. Osborne	*Miss P. Betz & Miss D. Hart*
1947	Miss D. Hart & Mrs. P. C. Todd	*Miss L. Brough & Miss M. Osborne*
1948	Miss L. Brough & Mrs. W. du Pont	*Miss D. Hart & Mrs. P. C. Todd*
1949	Miss L. Brough & Mrs. W. du Pont	*Miss G. Moran & Mrs. P. C. Todd*
1950	Miss L. Brough & Mrs. W. du Pont	*Miss S. Fry & Miss D. Hart*
1951	Miss S. Fry & Miss D. Hart	*Miss L. Brough & Mrs. W. du Pont*
1952	Miss S. Fry & Miss D. Hart	*Miss L. Brough & Miss M. Connolly*
1953	Miss S. Fry & Miss D. Hart	*Miss M. Connolly & Miss J. Sampson*
1954	Miss L. Brough & Mrs. W. du Pont	*Miss S. Fry & Miss D. Hart*
1955	Miss A. Mortimer & Miss J. A. Shilcock	*Miss S. J. Bloomer & Miss P. E. Ward*
1956	Miss A. Buxton & Miss A. Gibson	*Miss F. Muller & Miss D. G. Seeney*
1957	Miss A. Gibson & Miss D. R. Hard	*Mrs. K. Hawton & Mrs. T. D. Long*
1958	Miss M. E. Bueno & Miss A. Gibson	*Mrs. W. du Pont & Miss M. Varner*
1959	Miss J. Arth & Miss D. R. Hard	*Mrs. J. G. Fleitz & Miss C. C. Truman*
1960	Miss M. E. Bueno & Miss D. R. Hard	*Miss S. Reynolds & Miss R. Schuurman*
1961	Miss K. Hantze & Miss B. J. Moffitt	*Miss J. Lehane & Miss M. Smith*
1962	Miss B. J. Moffitt & Mrs. J. R. Susman	*Mrs. L. E. G. Price & Miss R. Schuurman*
1963	Miss M. E. Bueno & Miss D. R. Hard	*Miss R. A. Ebbern & Miss M. Smith*
1964	Miss M. Smith & Miss L. R. Turner	*Miss B. J. Moffitt & Mrs. J. R. Susman*
1965	Miss M. E. Bueno & Miss B. J. Moffitt	*Miss F. Durr & Miss J. LieVrig*
1966	Miss M. E. Bueno & Miss N. Richey	*Miss M. Smith & Miss J. A. M. Tegart*
1967	Miss R. Casals & Mrs. L. W. King	*Miss M. E. Bueno & Miss N. Richey*
1968	Miss R. Casals & Mrs. L. W. King	*Miss F. Durr & Mrs. P. F. Jones*
1969	Mrs. B. M. Court & Miss J. A. M. Tegart	*Miss P. S. A. Hogan & Miss M. Michel*
1970	Miss R. Casals & Mrs. L. W. King	*Miss F. Durr & Miss S. V. Wade*
1971	Miss R. Casals & Mrs. L. W. King	*Mrs. B. M. Court & Miss E. F. Goolagong*
1972	Mrs. L. W. King & Miss B. F. Stove	*Mrs. D. E. Dalton & Miss F. Durr*
1973	Miss R. Casals & Mrs. L. W. King	*Miss F. Durr & Miss B. F. Stove*
1974	Miss E. F. Goolagong & Miss M. Michel	*Miss H. F. Gourlay & Miss K. M. Krantzcke*
1975	Miss A. Kiyomura & Miss K. Sawamatsu	*Miss F. Durr & Miss B. F. Stove*
1976	Miss C. M. Evert & Miss M. Navratilova	*Mrs. L. W. King & Miss B. F. Stove*
1977	Mrs. H. F. Gourlay Cawley & Miss J. C. Russell	*Miss M. Navratilova & Miss B. F . Stove*
1978	Mrs. G. E. Reid & Miss. W. M. Turnbull	*Miss M. Jausovec & Miss V. Ruzici*
1979	Mrs. L. W. King & Miss M. Navratilova	*Miss B. F. Stove & Miss W. M. Turnbull*
1980	Miss K. Jordan & Miss A. E. Smith	*Miss R. Casals & Miss W. M. Turnbull*
1981	Miss M. Navratilova & Miss P. H. Shriver	*Miss K. Jordan & Miss A. E. Smith*
1982	Miss M. Navratilova & Miss P. H. Shriver	*Miss K. Jordan & Miss A. E. Smith*
1983	Miss M. Navratilova & Miss P. H. Shriver	*Miss R. Casals & Miss W. M. Turnbull*
1984	Miss M. Navratilova & Miss P. H. Shriver	*Miss K. Jordan & Miss A. E. Smith*
1985	Miss K. Jordan & Mrs. P. D. Smylie	*Miss M. Navratilova & Miss P. H. Shriver*
1986	Miss M. Navratilova & Miss P. H. Shriver	*Miss H. Mandlikova & Miss W. M. Turnbull*
1987	Miss C. Kohde-Kilsch & Miss H. Sukova	*Miss B. Nagelsen & Mrs. P. D. Smylie*
1988	Miss S. Graf & Miss G. Sabatini	*Miss L. Savchenko & Miss N. Zvereva*
1989	Miss J. Novotna & Miss H. Sukova	*Miss L. Savchenko & Miss N. Zvereva*
1990	Miss J. Novotna & Miss H. Sukova	*Miss K. Jordan & Mrs. P. D. Smylie*
1991	Miss L. Savchenko & Miss N. Zvereva	*Miss G. Fernandez & Miss J. Novotna*
1992	Miss G. Fernandez & Miss N. Zvereva	*Miss J. Novotna & Mrs. L. Savchenko-Neiland*
1993	Miss G. Fernandez & Miss N. Zvereva	*Mrs. L. Neiland & Miss J. Novotna*
1994	Miss G. Fernandez & Miss N. Zvereva	*Miss J. Novotna & Miss A. Sanchez Vicario*
1995	Miss J. Novotna & Miss A. Sanchez Vicario	*Miss G. Fernandez & Miss N. Zvereva*
1996	Miss M. Hingis & Miss H. Sukova	*Miss M.J. McGrath & Mrs. L. Neiland*
1997	Miss G. Fernandez & Miss N. Zvereva	*Miss N.J. Arendt & Miss M.M. Bollegraf*
1998	Miss M. Hingis & Miss J. Novotna	*Miss L.A. Davenport & Miss N. Zvereva*
1999	Miss L.A. Davenport & Miss C. Morariu	*Miss M. de Swardt & Miss E. Tatarkova*
2000	Miss S. Williams & Miss V. Williams	*Mrs J. Halard–Decugis & Miss A. Sugiyama*
2001	Miss L.M. Raymond & Miss R.P. Stubbs	*Miss K. Clijsters & Miss A. Sugiyama*
2002	Miss S. Williams & Miss V. Williams	*Miss V. Ruano Pascual & Miss P. Suarez*
2003	Miss K. Clijsters & Miss A. Sugiyama	*Miss V. Ruano Pascual & Miss P. Suarez*
2004	Miss C. Black & Miss R.P. Stubbs	*Mrs L. Huber & Miss A. Sugiyama*
2005	Miss C. Black & Mrs L. Huber	*Miss S. Kuznetsova & Miss A. Muresmo*
2006	Miss Z. Yan & Miss J. Zheng	*Miss V. Ruano Pascual & Miss P. Suarez*
2007	Miss C. Black & Mrs L. Huber	*Miss K. Srebotnik & Miss A. Sugiyama*
2008	Miss S. Williams & Miss V. Williams	*Miss L. M. Raymond & Miss S. Stosur*

1913 H. Crisp and Mrs. C. O. Tuckey
J. C. Parke and Mrs. D. R. Larcombe

1914 J. C. Parke and Mrs. D.R. Larcombe
A. F. Wilding and Mlle. M. Broquedis

1919 R. Lycett and Miss E. Ryan
A. D. Prebble and Mrs. Lambert Chambers

1920 G. L. Patterson and Mlle. S. Lenglen
R. Lycett and Miss E. Ryan

1921 R. Lycett and Miss E. Ryan
M. Woosnam and Miss P. L. Howkins

1922 P. O'Hara-Wood and Mlle. S. Lenglen
R. Lycett and Miss E. Ryan

1923 R. Lycett and Miss E. Ryan
L. S. Deane and Mrs. D. C. Shepherd-Barron

1924 J. B. Gilbert and Miss K. McKane
L. A. Godfree and Mrs. D. C. Shepherd-Barron

1925 J. Borotra and Mlle. S. Lenglen
H. L. de Morpurgo and Miss E. Ryan

1926 L. A. Godfree and Mrs. L. A. Godfree
H. Kinsey and Miss M. K. Browne

1927 F. T. Hunter and Miss E. Ryan
L. A. Godfree and Mrs. L. A. Godfree

1928 P. D. B. Spence and Miss E. Ryan
J. Crawford and Miss D. Akhurst

1929 F. T. Hunter and Miss H. Wills
I. G. Collins and Miss J. Fry

1930 J. H. Crawford and Miss E. Ryan
D. Prenn and Fraulein H. Krahwinkel

1931 G. M. Lott and Mrs L. A. Harper
I. G. Collins and Miss J. C. Ridley

1932 E. Maier and Miss E. Ryan
H. C. Hopman and Mlle. J. Sigart

1933 G. von Cramm and Fraulein H. Krahwinkel
N. G. Farquharson and Miss M. Heeley

1934 R. Miki and Miss D. E. Round
H. W. Austin and Mrs D. C. Shepherd-Barron

1935 F. J. Perry and Miss D. E. Round
H. C. Hopman and Mrs. H. C. Hopman

1936 F. J. Perry and Miss D. E. Round
J. D. Budge and Mrs. S. P. Fabyan

1937 J. D. Budge and Miss A. Marble
Y. Petra and Mme. R. Mathieu

1938 J. D. Budge and Miss A. Marble
H. Henkel and Mrs. S. P. Fabyan

1939 R. L. Riggs and Miss A. Marble
F. H. D. Wilde and Miss N. B. Brown

1946 T. Brown and Miss L. Brough
G. E. Brown and Miss D. Bundy

1947 J. E. Bromwich and Miss L. Brough
C. F. Long and Mrs. N. M. Bolton

1948 J. E. Bromwich and Miss L. Brough
F. A. Sedgman and Miss D. Hart

1949 E. W. Sturgess and Mrs. S. P. Summers
J. E. Bromwich and Miss L. Brough

1950 E. W. Sturgess and Miss L. Brough
G. E. Brown and Mrs. P. C. Todd

1951 F. A. Sedgman and Miss D. Hart
M. G. Rose and Mrs. N. M. Bolton

1952 F. A. Sedgman and Miss D. Hart
E. Morea and Mrs. T. D. Long

1953 V. Seixas and Miss D. Hart
E. Morea and Miss S. Fry

1954 V. Seixas and Miss D. Hart
K. R. Rosewall and Mrs. W. du Pont

1955 V. Seixas and Miss D. Hart
E. Morea and Miss L. Brough

1956 V. Seixas and Miss S. Fry
G. Mulloy and Miss A. Gibson

1957 M. G. Rose and Miss D. R. Hard
N. A. Fraser and Miss A. Gibson

1958 R. N. Howe and Miss L. Coghlan
K. Nielsen and Miss A. Gibson

1959 R. Laver and Miss D. R. Hard
N. A. Fraser and Miss M. E. Bueno

1960 R. Laver and Miss D. R. Hard
R. N. Howe and Miss M. E. Bueno

1961 F. S. Stolle and Miss L. R. Turner
R. N. Howe and Miss E. Buding

1962 N. A. Fraser and Mrs. W. du Pont
R. D. Ralston and Miss A. S. Haydon

1963 K. N. Fletcher and Miss M. Smith
R. A. J. Hewitt and Miss D. R. Hard

1964 F. S. Stolle and Miss L. R. Turner
K. N. Fletcher and Miss M. Smith

1965 K. N. Fletcher and Miss M. Smith
A. D. Roche and Miss J. A. M. Tegart

1966 K. N. Fletcher and Miss M. Smith
R. D. Ralston amd Mrs. L. W. King

1967 O. K. Davidson and Mrs. L. W. King
K. N. Fletcher and Miss M. E. Bueno

1968 K. N. Fletcher and Mrs. B. M. Court
A. Metreveli and Miss O. Morozova

1969 F. S. Stolle and Mrs. P. F. Jones
A. D. Roche and Miss J. A. M. Tegart

1970 I. Nastase and Miss R. Casals
A. Metreveli and Miss O. Morozova

1971 O. K. Davidson and Mrs. L. W. King
M. C. Riessen and Mrs. B. M. Court

1972 I. Nastase and Miss R. Casals
K.G. Warwick and Miss E. F. Goolagong

1973 O. K. Davidson and Mrs. L. W. King
R. Ramirez and Miss J. S. Newberry

1974 O. K. Davidson and Mrs. L. W. King
M. J. Farrell and Miss L. J. Charles

1975 M. C. Riessen and Mrs. B. M. Court
A. J. Stone and Miss B. F. Stove

1976 A. D. Roche and Miss F. Durr
R. L. Stockton and Miss R. Casals

1977 R. A. J. Hewitt and Miss G. R. Stevens
F. D. McMillan and Miss B. F. Stove

1978 F. D. McMillan and Miss B. F. Stove
R. O. Ruffels and Mrs. L. W. King

1979 R. A. J. Hewitt and Miss G. R. Stevens
F. D. McMillan and Miss B. F. Stove

1980 J. R. Austin and Miss T. Austin
M. R. Edmondson and Miss D. L. Fromholtz

1981 F. D. McMillan and Miss B. F. Stove
J. R. Austin and Miss T. Austin

1982 K. Curren and Miss A. E. Smith
J. M. Lloyd and Miss W. M. Turnbull

1983 J. M. Lloyd and Miss W. M. Turnbull
S. Denton and Mrs. L. W. King

1984 J. M. Lloyd and Miss W. M. Turnbull
S. Denton and Miss K. Jordan

1985 P. McNamee and Miss M. Navratilova
J. B. Fitzgerald and Mrs. P. D. Smylie

1986 K. Flach and Miss K. Jordan
H. P. Guenthardt and Miss M. Navratilova

1987 M. J. Bates and Miss J. M. Durie
D. Cahill and Miss N. Provis

1988 S. E. Stewart and Miss Z. L. Garrison
K. Jones and Mrs. S. W. Magers

1989 J. Pugh and Miss J. Novotna
M. Kratzmann and Miss J. M. Byrne

1990 R. Leach and Miss Z. L. Garrison
J. B. Fitzgerald and Mrs P. D. Smylie

1991 J. B. Fitzgerald and Mrs. P. D. Smylie
J. Pugh and Miss N. Zvereva

1992 C. Suk and Mrs L. Savchenko-Neiland
J. Eltingh and Miss M. Oremans

1993 M. Woodforde and Miss M. Navratilova
T. Nijssen and Miss M. M. Bollegraf

1994 T. A. Woodbridge and Miss H. Sukova
T. J. Middleton and Miss L. M. McNeil

1995 J. Stark and Miss M. Navratilova
C. Suk and Miss G. Fernandez

1996 C. Suk and Miss H. Sukova
M. Woodforde and Mrs. L. Neiland

1997 C. Suk and Miss H. Sukova
A. Olhovskiy and Mrs L. Neiland

1998 M. Mirnyi and Miss S. Williams
M. Bhupathi and Miss M. Lucic

1999 L. Paes and Miss L.M. Raymond
J. Bjorkman and Miss A. Kournikova

2000 D. Johnson and Miss K. Po
L. Hewitt and Miss K. Clijsters

2001 L. Friedl and Miss D. Hantuchova
M. Bryan and Mrs L. Huber

2002 M. Bhupathi and Miss E. Likhovtseva
K. Ullyett and Miss D. Hantuchova

2003 L. Paes and Miss M. Navratilova
A. Ram and Miss A. Rodionova

2004 W. Black and Miss C. Black
T.A. Woodbridge and Miss A. Molik

2005 M. Bhupathi and Miss M. Pierce
P. Hanley and Miss T. Perebiynis

2006 A. Ram and Miss V. Zvonareva
B. Bryan and Miss V. Williams

2007 J. Murray & Miss J. Jankovic
J. Bjorkman & Miss A. Molik

2008 B. Bryan & Miss S. Stosur
M. Bryan & Miss K. Srebotnik

THE CHAMPIONSHIP ROLL

BOYS' SINGLES

1947 K. Nielsen (Denmark)
S. V. Davidson (Sweden)
1948 S. Stockenberg (Sweden)
D. Vad (Hungary)
1949 S. Stockenberg (Sweden)
J. A.T. Horn (G.B.)
1950 J. A.T. Horn (G.B.)
K. Mobarek (Egypt)
1951 J. Kupferburger (S.A.)
K. Mobarek (Egypt)
1952 R. K. Wilson (G.B.)
T. T. Fancutt (S.A.)
1953 W. A. Knight (G.B.)
R. Krishnan (India)
1954 R. Krishnan (India)
A. J. Cooper (Australia)
1955 M. P. Hann (G.B.)
J. E. Lundquist (Sweden)
1956 R. Holmberg (U.S.A.)
R. G. Laver (Australia)
1957 J. I. Tattersall (G.B.)
I. Ribeiro (Brazil)
1958 E. Buchholz (U.S.A.)
P. J. Lall (India)
1959 T. Lejus (U.S.S.R.)
R. W. Barnes (Brazil)
1960 A. R. Mandelstam (S.A.)
J. Mukerjea (India)
1961 C. E. Graebner (U.S.A.)
E. Blanke (Austria)

1962 S. Matthews (G.B.)
A. Metreveli (U.S.S.R.)
1963 N. Kalogeropoulos (Greece)
I. El Shafei (U.A.R.)
1964 I. El Shafei (U.A.R.)
V. Korotkov (U.S.S.R.)
1965 V. Korotkov (U.S.S.R.)
G. Goven (France)
1966 V. Korotkov (U.S.S.R.)
B. E. Fairlie (N.Z.)
1967 M. Orantes (Spain)
M. S. Estep (U.S.A.)
1968 J. G. Alexander (Australia)
J. Thamin (France)
1969 B. Bertram (S.A.)
J. G. Alexander (Australia)
1970 B. Bertram (S.A.)
F. Gebert (Germany)
1971 R. Kreiss (U.S.A.)
S. A. Warboys (G.B.)
1972 B. Borg (Sweden)
C. J. Mottram (G.B.)
1973 W. Martin (U.S.A.)
C. S. Dowdeswell (Rhodesia)
1974 W. Martin (U.S.A.)
Ash Amritraj (India)
1975 C. J. Lewis (N.Z.)
R. Ycaza (Ecuador)
1976 H. Guenthardt (Switzerland)
P. Elter (Germany)
1977 V. A. Winitsky (U.S.A.)
T. E. Teltscher (U.S.A.)

1978 I. Lendl (Czechoslovakia)
J. Turpin (U.S.A.)
1979 R. Krishnan (India)
D. Siegler (U.S.A.)
1980 T. Tulasne (France)
H. D. Beutel (Germany)
1981 M. W. Anger (U.S.A.)
P. Cash (Australia)
1982 P. Cash (Australia)
H. Sundstrom (Sweden)
1983 S. Edberg (Sweden)
J. Frawley (Australia)
1984 M.Kratzmann (Australia)
S. Kruger (S.A.)
1985 L. Lavalle (Mexico)
E. Velez (Mexico)
1986 E. Velez (Mexico)
J. Sanchez (Spain)
1987 D. Nargiso (Italy)
J. R. Stoltenberg (Australia)
1988 N. Pereira (Venezuela)
G. Raoux (France)
1989 N. Kulti (Sweden)
T. A. Woodbridge (Australia)
1990 L. Paes (India)
M. Ondruska (S.A.)
1991 T. Enquist (Sweden)
M. Joyce (U.S.A.)
1992 D. Skoch (Czechoslovakia)
B. Dunn (U.S.A.)
1993 R. Sabau (Romania)
J. Szymanski (Venezuela)

1994 S. Humphries (U.S.A.)
M. A. Philippoussis (Australia)
1995 O. Mutis (France)
N. Kiefer (Germany)
1996 V. Voltchkov (Belarus)
I. Ljubicic (Croatia)
1997 W. Whitehouse (S.A.)
D. Elsner (Germany)
1998 R. Federer (Switzerland)
I. Labadze (Georgia)
1999 J. Melzer (Austria)
K. Pless (Denmark)
2000 N. Mahut (France)
M. Ancic (Croatia)
2001 R. Valent (Switzerland)
G. Muller (Luxembourg)
2002 T. Reid (Australia)
L. Quahab (Algeria)
2003 F. Mergea (Romania)
C. Guccione (Australia)
2004 G. Monfils (France)
M. Kasiri (G.B.)
2005 J. Chardy (France)
R. Haase (Netherlands)
2006 T. De Bakker (Netherlands)
M. Gawron (Poland)
2007 D. Young (U.S.A)
V. Ignatic (Belarus)
2008 G. Dimitrov (Bulgaria)
H. Kontinen (Finland)

BOYS' DOUBLES

1982 P. Cash & J. Frawley
R. D. Leach & J. J. Ross
1983 M. Kratzmann & S. Youl
M. Nastase & O. Rahnasto
1984 R. Brown & R. Weiss
M. Kratzmann & J. Svensson
1985 A. Moreno & J. Yzaga
P. Korda & C. Suk
1986 T. Carbonell & P. Korda
S. Barr & H. Karrasch
1987 J. Stoltenberg & T. Woodbridge
D. Nargiso & E. Rossi
1988 J. Stoltenberg & T. Woodbridge
D. Rikl & T. Zdrazila

1989 J. Palmer & J. Stark
J-L. De Jager & W. R. Ferreira
1990 S. Lareau & S. Leblanc
C. Marsh & M. Ondruska
1991 K. Alami & G. Rusedski
J-L. De Jager & A. Medvedev
1992 S. Baldas & S. Draper
M. S. Bhupathi & N. Kirtane
1993 S. Downs & J. Greenhalgh
N. Godwin & G. Williams
1994 B. Ellwood & M. Philippoussis
V. Platenik & R. Schlachter
1995 M. Lee & J.M. Trotman
A. Hernandez & M. Puerta

1996 D. Bracciali & J. Robichaud
D. Roberts & W. Whitehouse
1997 L. Horna & N. Massu
J. Van de Westhuizen & W. Whitehouse
1998 R. Federer & O. Rochus
M. Llodra & A. Ram
1999 G. Coria & D. Nalbandian
T. Enev & J. Nieminem
2000 D. Coene & K. Vliegen
A. Banks & B. Riby
2001 F. Dancevic & G. Lapentti
B. Echagaray & S. Gonzales
2002 F. Mergea & H. Tecau
B. Baker & B. Ram

2003 F. Mergea & H. Tecau
A. Feeney & C. Guccione
2004 B. Evans & S. Oudsema
R. Haase & V. Troicki
2005 J. Levine & M. Shabaz
S. Groth & A. Kennaugh
2006 K. Damico & N. Schnugg
M. Klizan & A. Martin
2007 D. Lopez & M. Trevisan
R. Jebavy & M. Klizan
2008 Cheng-Peng Hsieh & Tsung-Hua Yang
M. Reid & B. Tomic

GIRLS' SINGLES

1947 Miss G. Domken (Belgium)
Miss B. Wallen (Sweden)
1948 Miss O. Miskova (Czechoslovakia)
Miss V. Rigollet (Switzerland)
1949 Miss C. Mercelis (Belgium)
Miss J. S. V. Partridge (G.B.)
1950 Miss L. Cornell (G.B.)
Miss A. Winter (Norway)
1951 Miss L. Cornell (G.B.)
Miss S. Lazzarino (Italy)
1952 Miss F. J. I. ten Bosch (Netherlands)
Miss R. Davar (India)
1953 Miss D. Kilian (S.A.)
Miss V. A. Pitt (G.B.)
1954 Miss V. A. Pitt (G.B.)
Miss C. Monnot (France)
1955 Miss S. M. Armstrong (G.B.)
Miss B. de Chambure (France)
1956 Miss A. S. Haydon (G.B.)
Miss I. Buding (Germany)
1957 Miss M. Arnold (U.S.A.)
Miss E. Reyes (Mexico)
1958 Miss S. M. Moore (U.S.A)
Miss A. Dmitrieva (U.S.S.R.)
1959 Miss J. Cross (S.A.)
Miss D. Schuster (Austria)
1960 Miss K. Hantze (U.S.A)
Miss L. M. Hutchings (S.A.)
1961 Miss G. Baksheeva (U.S.S.R.)
Miss K. D. Chabot (U.S.A.)
1962 Miss G. Baksheeva (U.S.S.R.)
Miss E. P. Terry (N.Z.)

1963 Miss D. M. Salfati (France)
Miss K. Dening (Australia)
1964 Miss P. Bartkowicz (U.S.A)
Miss E. Subirats (Mexico)
1965 Miss O. Morozova (U.S.S.R.)
Miss R. Giscarfe (Argentina)
1966 Miss B. Lindstrom (Finland)
Miss J. A. Congdon (G.B.)
1967 Miss J. Salome (Netherlands)
Miss E. M. Strandberg (Sweden)
1968 Miss K. Pigeon (U.S.A)
Miss L. E. Hunt (Australia)
1969 Miss K. Sawamatsu (Japan)
Miss B. I. Kirk (S.A.)
1970 Miss S. Walsh (U.S.A)
Miss M. V. Kroshina (U.S.S.R.)
1971 Miss M.V. Kroschina (U.S.S.R.)
Miss S. H. Minford (G.B.)
1972 Miss I. Kloss (S.A.)
Miss G. L. Coles (G.B.)
1973 Miss A. Kiyomura (U.S.A)
Miss M. Navratilova (Czechoslovakia)
1974 Miss M. Jausovec (Yugoslavia)
Miss M. Simionescu (Romania)
1975 Miss N. Y. Chmyreva (U.S.S.R.)
Miss R. Marsikova (Czechoslovakia)
1976 Miss N. Y. Chmyreva (U.S.S.R.)
Miss M. Kruger (S.A.)
1977 Miss L. Antonoplis (U.S.A)
Miss Mareen Louie (U.S.A.)
1978 Miss T. Austin (U.S.A)
Miss H. Mandlikova (Czechoslovakia)

1979 Miss M. L. Piatek (U.S.A)
Miss A. A. Moulton (U.S.A.)
1980 Miss D. Freeman (Australia)
Miss S. J. Leo (Australia)
1981 Miss Z. Garrison (U.S.A)
Miss R. R. Uys (S.A.)
1982 Miss C. Tanvier (France)
Miss H. Sukova (Czechoslovakia)
1983 Miss P. Paradis (France)
Miss P. Hy (Hong Kong)
1984 Miss A. N. Croft (G.B.)
Miss E. Reinach (S.A.)
1985 Miss A. Holikova (Czechoslovakia)
Miss J. M. Byrne (Australia)
1986 Miss N.M. Zvereva (U.S.S.R.)
Miss L. Meskhi (U.S.S.R.)
1987 Miss N.M. Zvereva (U.S.S.R.)
Miss J. Halard (France)
1988 Miss B. Schultz (Netherlands)
Miss E. Derly (France)
1989 Miss A. Strnadova (Czechoslavakia)
Miss M. J. McGrath (U.S.A.)
1990 Miss A. Strnadova (Czechoslavakia)
Miss K. Sharpe (Australia)
1991 Miss B. Rittner (Germany)
Miss E. Makarova (U.S.S.R.)
1992 Miss C. Rubin (U.S.A)
Miss L. Courtois (Belgium)
1993 Miss N. Feber (Belgium)
Miss R. Grande (Italy)
1994 Miss M. Hingis (Switzerland)
Miss M-R. Jeon (Korea)

1995 Miss A. Olsza (Poland)
Miss T. Tanasugarn (Thailand)
1996 Miss A. Mauresmo (France)
Miss M. L. Serna (Spain)
1997 Miss C. Black (Zimbabwe)
Miss A. Rippner (U.S.A.)
1998 Miss K. Srebotnik (Slovenia)
Miss K. Clijsters (Belgium)
1999 Miss I. Tulyagnova (Uzbekhistan)
Miss L. Krasnoroutskaya (U.S.S.R.)
2000 Miss M. E. Salerni (Argentina)
Miss T. Perebiynis (Ukraine)
2001 Miss A. Widjaja (Indonesia)
Miss D. Safina (U.S.S.R.)
2002 Miss V. Douchevina (Russia)
Miss M. Sharapova (U.S.S.R.)
2003 Miss K. Flipkens (Belgium)
Miss A. Tchakvetadze (U.S.S.R.)
2004 Miss A. Bondarenko (Ukraine)
Miss A. Ivanovic (Serbia and Montenegro)
2005 Miss A. Radwanska (Poland)
Miss T. Paszek (Austria)
2006 Miss C. Wozniacki (Denmark)
Miss M. Rybarikova (Slovakia)
2007 Miss U. Radwanska (Poland)
Miss M. Brengle (U.S.A)
2008 Miss L. Robson (G.B.)
Miss N. Lertcheewakarn (Thailand)

GIRLS' DOUBLES

1982 Miss B. Herr & Miss P. Barg
Miss B. S. Gerken & Miss G. A. Rush
1983 Miss P. Fendick & Miss P. Hy
Miss C. Anderholm & Miss H. Olsson
1984 Miss C. Kuhlman & Miss S. Rehe
Miss V. Milvidskaya & Miss L.I. Savchenko
1985 Miss L. Field & Miss J. Thompson
Miss E. Reinach & Miss J. A. Richardson
1986 Miss M. Jaggard & Miss L. O'Neill
Miss L. Meskhi & Miss N.M. Zvereva
1987 Miss N. Medvedeva & Miss N.M. Zvereva
Miss I. S. Kim & Miss P. M. Moreno
1988 Miss J. A. Faull & Miss R. McQuillan
Miss A. Dechaume & Miss E. Derly

1989 Miss J. Capriati & Miss M. McGrath
Miss A. Strnadova & Miss E. Sviglerova
1990 Miss K. Habsudova & Miss A. Strnadova
Miss N. J. Pratt & Miss K. Sharpe
1991 Miss C. Barclay & Miss L. Zaltz
Miss J. Limmer & Miss A. Woolcock
1992 Miss M. Avotins & Miss L. McShea
Miss P. Nelson & Miss J. Steven
1993 Miss L. Courtois & Miss N. Feber
Miss H. Mochizuki & Miss Y. Yoshida
1994 Miss E. De Villiers & Miss E. E. Jelfs
Miss C. M. Morariu & Miss L. Varmuzova
1995 Miss C. Black & Miss A. Olsza
Miss T. Musgrove & Miss J Richardson

1996 Miss O. Barabanschikova &
Miss A. Mauresmo
Miss L. Osterloh & Miss S. Reeves
1997 Miss C. Black & Miss I. Selyutina
Miss M. Matevzic & Miss K. Srebotnik
1998 Miss E. Dyrberg & Miss J. Kostanic
Miss P. Rampre & Miss I. Tulyagonova
1999 Miss D. Bedanova & Miss M.E. Salerni
Miss T. Perebiynis & Miss I. Tulyaganova
2000 Miss I. Gaspar & Miss T. Perebiynis
Miss D. Bedanova & Miss M. E. Salerni
2001 Miss G. Dulko & Miss A. Harkleroad
Miss C. Horiatopoulos & Miss B. Mattek

2002 Miss E. Clijsters & Miss B. Strycova
Miss A. Baker & Miss A-L. Groenfeld
2003 Miss A. Kleybanova & Miss S. Mirza
Miss K. Bohmova & Miss M. Krajicek
2004 Miss V. Azarenka & Miss V. Havartsova
Miss M. Erakovic & Miss M. Niculescu
2005 Miss V. Azarenka & Miss A. Szavay
Miss M. Erakovic & Miss M. Niculescu
2006 Miss A. Kleybanova & Miss A. Pavlyuchenkova
Miss A. Antoniychuk & Miss A. Dulgheru
2007 Miss A. Pavlyuchenkova & Miss U. Radwanska
Miss M. Doi & Miss K. Nara
2008 Miss P. Hercog & Miss J. Moore
Miss I. Holland & Miss S. Peers